# BRAZILIAN POETRY (1950–1980)

WESLEYAN POETRY

# BRAZILIAN POETRY (1950–1980)

Edited, with an Introduction, by EMANUEL BRASIL
and WILLIAM JAY SMITH

WESLEYAN UNIVERSITY PRESS
MIDDLETOWN, CONNECTICUT

The publishers are grateful to the Translation Center, Columbia University, and the Center for Inter-American Relations and Ms. Rosario Santos, without whose assistance this anthology would not have been possible.

Acknowledgment is also made to the following:

The Brazilian poets, their heirs, and their publishers who have generously given permission for their works to be included in this anthology;

*An Anthology of Concrete Poetry,* edited by Emmett Williams, Something Else Press, Inc. 1967, copyright © 1967 for "Sevidão de passagem" ("Transient Servitude") and for the Notes by Haroldo de Campos;

Carcanet Press for Edwin Morgan's translation of "Transient Servitude" by Haroldo de Campos, from *Rites of Passage: Selected Translations* by Edwin Morgan, published by Carcanet Press, 1976, copyright © 1976 by Carcanet New Press. Reprinted by permission.

*The Literary Review* (Winter 1978), Farleigh Dickinson University, for "Dionysus in Brazil" by Jorge Mautner, translated by Romney Meyran.

Edwin Morgan for his translation of "Eixo," by Augusto de Campos.

Illustration for "The Tiger" of Blake: From a Dervish mural, Turkey, 19th century. The letters in the body of the tiger compose a Mohammedan inscription, which means, in part: "In the name of the lion of God, of the face of God, of triumphant Ali son of Ebu Talet." (T. K. Birge, *The Bektashi Order of Dervishes,* London, 1952, mentioned by Berjouhl Bowler in *The Word as Image,* London, Studio Vista Ltd., 1970.)

Published by Wesleyan University Press, 110 Mt. Vernon Street, Middletown, Connecticut 06457

Distributed by Harper & Row, Publishers, Keystone Industrial Park, Scranton, Pennsylvania 18512

Manufactured in the United States of America
First Edition

ISBN: 0-8195-5075-2 cloth
ISBN: 0-8195-6083-0 paper

To the memory of ELIZABETH BISHOP

# CONTENTS

Introduction 2

Dionysus in Brazil 9

JORGE MAUTNER (1941– ) was born in São Paulo. He is a poet, musician, singer, composer, and showman. His first book was *God of Rain and Death (Deus da Chuva e da Morte)* (1962) and his most recent is *Poetry of Love and Death (Poesias de Amor e de Morte)* (1982). As a composer-singer, he has several albums—*Bomb of Stars (Bomba de Estrelas)* is his most recent one—and many stage appearances throughout Brazil to his credit.

A Casa / The House 10

As Peras / The Pears 14

Coisas da Terra / Things of the Earth 18

Agosto 1964 / August 1964 20

Oswald Morto / Oswald Dead 22

Bananas Podres / Rotten Bananas 24

Um Sorriso / A Smile 46

Subversiva / Subversive 48

Homem Sentado / Man Seated 50

FERREIRA GULLAR (JOSÉ RIBAMAR FERREIRÁ), poet, playwright, essayist, art critic, and journalist, was born in 1930 in São Luís do Maranhão. In 1951 he moved to Rio. His first book *The Bodily Struggle (A Luta Corporal)* (1954) established his reputation as a poet who could write with precision about down-to-earth matters. Until 1962 he was in the forefront of the avant-garde. He then began to concentrate more seriously on social problems. An opponent of the military regime established in 1964, he went into exile in 1971, and returned to Brazil only in 1977. In that year he published his *Dirty Poem (Poema Sujo)*, which celebrates every aspect of his native city. He now earns his living as an art critic and as a writer for television.

## CONTENTS

HAROLDO DE CAMPOS (1929– ) was born in São Paulo, and is Professor of Literary Theory at the Catholic Pontifical University there. In 1972 he received a Guggenheim Fellowship and in 1978 was Fulbright-Hays Visiting Professor in the Department of Spanish and Portuguese at Yale University. With his brother Augusto and Décio Pignatari, he founded the *Noigandres* group and helped launch the international movement of concrete poetry. In addition to his work in the *Noigandres* collections, he has published many books, including *Auto of the Possessed (Auto do Possesso)* (1950) and *Transient Servitude (Servidão de Passagem)* (1962). He has translated works of Dante, Pound, Joyce, Mallarmé, Mayakovsky, and Khlebnikov.


**Servidão de Passagem / Transient Servitude** 52
**Proem**
**Poem**
**Note**

**Esboços para uma Nékuia / Sketches for a Nekuia** 58
**Notes**


MÁRIO FAUSTINO (DOS SANTOS E SILVA) (1930–1962) was born in Teresina (Piauí). He wrote his first poems at the age of sixteen. He studied law in Pará and language and literature at Pomona College, California. In 1953 he traveled in Europe. His only book of poems *Man and His Time (O Homem e Sua Hora)* was published in 1955. From 1956 to 1958 he edited in the Sunday supplement of the Rio periodical *Jornal do Brasil* an influential page of poetic analysis and appreciation entitled *Poetry-Experiment (Poesia-Experiência)*. He worked at the United Nations in New York in 1959 and as a journalist on his return to Brazil in 1960. He died in an airplane accident in 1962.


**Prefácio / Preface** 86

**Sinto Que o Mês Presente Me Assassina / This Month Will Kill Me I Feel It** 88

**Vida Toda Linguagem / Life Nothing but Language** 90

**Juventude— / Youth—** 92

**Cavossonante Escudo Nosso / Our Hollow-sounding Shield** 96

**Moriturus Salutat / Moriturus Salutat** 100

**Ariazul / Blue Aria** 104

## CONTENTS

AUGUSTO DE CAMPOS (1931–    ) was born in São Paulo. With his brother Haroldo and Décio Pignatari he founded the *Noigandres* group and was one of the principal initiators of the international Concretist movement. His color poems *(Poetamenos)* (1953) are considered the first examples of concrete poetry in Brazil. With other poets and painters he organized the First National Exhibition of Concrete Art at the Museum of Modern Art in São Paulo in 1956, and participated later in many international exhibitions. In addition to contributing concrete poems to the literary magazines *Noigandres* and *Invenção*, which he helped to edit, he is the author of *The King Minus the Kingdom (O Rei Menos O Reino)* (1951) and of *Poems 1949–1979 (Poesia 1949–1979)* (1979). He has translated works of Cummings, Pound, and Joyce, and with his brother was visiting lecturer at the Universities of Texas, Indiana, and Wisconsin in 1968.


**Eixo / Axis** 109

**Ôlho Por Ôlho / Eye for Eye** 110

**Tudo Está Dito / Everything Was Said** 111

**O Pulsar / The Pulsar** 114

**O Quasar / The Quasar** 117

**Memos / Memos** 120

**A Rosa Doente / The Sick Rose** 122

**O Tygre / The Tyger** 124 125

**Pentahexagrama para John Cage / Pentahexagram for John Cage** 134


DÉCIO PIGNATARI (1927–    ) was born in São Paulo, where he took a Ph.D. in literary theory at the University in 1973. He was co-founder of *Noigandres* magazine with Haroldo and Augusto de Campos and of the subsequent Concretist movement (1956). He was editor of *Invenção* (1962–1967) and co-editor of *Através* (begun in 1977). With Haroldo and Augusto de Campos he wrote *Theory of Concrete Poetry (Teoria de Poesia Concreta)* (1965) and translated selections from Ezra Pound's *Cantos*. His poems have appeared in international magazines and anthologies; and he has published essays and books on communication, semiotics, poetics, art, architecture, and literary criticism. Graphic artist and "language designer," he has taught information theory at Brasilia University and at the School of Industrial Design in Rio de Janeiro.


**Noosfera / Noûsphere** 136

**Beba Coca Cola / Drink Coca-Cola** 138

**Life / Life** 140

**Cr$isto é a solução / Chr$ist is the Answer** 146

## CONTENTS

LINDOLF BELL (1938–    ) was born in Timbó, Santa Catarina. He graduated in drama from the Escola de Arte Dramática of São Paulo under the direction of Alfredo Mesquita. He took part in the International Writing Program at the University of Iowa (1968–1969) and taught art history in 1975 at the Universidade Regional of Blumenau, Santa Catarina. In 1964 he started a literary movement called "Catequese Poetica" ("Poetical Catechism"), taking poetry to the streets, and to stadiums, factories, universities, bars, and other public places. In 1974 he printed poems on T-shirts and called them *Corpoemas (Body Poems)*. He also printed poster poems and in 1981 created in Santa Catarina the first Square of the Poem with poems engraved on large stones. In 1981 also he received the Miguel de Cervantes Prize from the state of São Paulo, which enabled him to travel to Spain and Portugal.

**Poema a um Jovem / Poem to a Young Man** 148

**Retrato de um Ex-jovem Burguês / Portrait of an Ex-Young Bourgeois** 150

**O Poema das Crianças Traídas / Poem of the Betrayed Children** 154

**Das Circunstâncias do Poema / On a Poem's Circumstances** 156

**O Portão da Casa / The House Gate** 160

**Da Esperança / On Hope** 164

**Minifúndio / Small Farm** 168

**Desterro / Exile** 170

**Deste Âmago Provo o Amargo Gosto / Of This Core I Sample the Bitter Taste** 172

**Do Tempo / On Time** 174

**O Poema do Telhado de Vidro / The Glass Roof Poem** 176

**Bibliography** 184

**Notes on Editors and Translators** 186

# BRAZILIAN POETRY (1950–1980)

## INTRODUCTION

The six poets whose work is collected for the first time in this anthology came into prominence in the nineteen-fifties and sixties and have dominated poetry in Brazil ever since. To understand fully the impact of their arrival on the literary scene, we should first review some of the significant developments in the poetry of that country earlier in the century.

The year 1922, which marked the centennial of Brazilian independence, was also a year of importance for the development of modern art, and particularly modern poetry, in Brazil. A group of writers and artists organized "Modern Art Week" in February of that year in São Paulo. This celebration, during which the group set forth the avant-garde ideas that they had adopted in France and Italy, became as much a landmark in Brazilian culture as the New York Armory Show of 1913 is in the culture of the United States.

The poet Menotti del Pichia presented the artistic aim of the group in these words: "We want light, air, ventilators, airplanes, workers' demands, idealism, motors, factory smokestacks, blood, speed, dream, in our Art. And may the chugging of an automobile, on the track of two lines of verse, frighten away from poetry the last Homeric god who went on sleeping and dreaming of the flutes of Arcadian shepherds and the divine breasts of Helen, an anachronism in the era of the jazz band and the movie." The Modernist poetic movement, repudiating French and Portuguese influences, rejected the ideas of the Romantics, Parnassians, and Symbolists, and attempted to use with complete honesty the materials of everyday life. Mário de Andrade (1893–1945), a leader of the Modernist group, was one of the first intellectuals to become seriously interested in the immense untapped resources of Brazilian folklore and modern music. Manuel Bandeira (1886–1968) wrote a poem entitled "Brazilian Tragedy," which concerned the murder of a syphilitic prostitute. But the most radical member of the group was Oswald de Andrade (1890–1953), who published in Paris in 1925 an important book of poems called *Brazilwood (Pau Brasil).* Born into a wealthy family, Oswald de Andrade had returned from Europe in 1912 with a copy of Marinetti's *Futurist Manifesto.* He created a sensation at the time by publishing a poem without rhyme or meter, entitled "Last Ride of a Tubercular through the City by Streetcar." In *Brazilwood* he treated in simple language Brazilian themes, customs, superstitions, and family life. For the first time in Brazilian poetry he wrote of serious subjects with wit and humor. Like e. e. cummings he used the language of modern advertisements for satiric purposes; his poem "National Library" is simply a list of book titles placed incongruously side by side. The qualities that Oswald de Andrade espoused have marked Brazilian poetry ever since, and without him and the other poets of *modernismo* the work of the poets of the fifties and sixties would not have been possible. In his poem "Oswald Dead" *(Oswald Morto),* Ferreira Gullar pays tribute to the poet "who prophesied the leisure civilization" with its attendant irony:

The faster you go the idler you get.

The year 1945 marked another pronounced shift in poetic styles. That year brought the dropping of the first atomic bomb, about which every Brazilian poet seems to have written, and the end of World War II. It also brought the death of Mário de Andrade and the appearance of a new generation of poets, the Neo-Modernists, or the generation of '45. This new group reacted against the exaggerated use of free verse and wanted poetry to be more precise and less sentimental. João Cabral de Melo Neto (1920– ), whose work is characterized by striking visual imagery derived for the most part from his native northeast, came to prominence with this generation, and has continued to be a dominant figure since that time.

In 1954 João Cabral de Melo Neto published his *Collected Poems (Poemas Reunidos).* The early fifties saw the publication of other books that signaled the final flowering of the Modernist movement. In 1951 appeared *Clear Enigma (Claro Enigma)* by Carlos Drummond de Andrade (1902– ), considered the most important of the older generation of poets. He was born in the little town of Itabirito in the state of Minas Gerais. As his name indicates, he has Scottish blood, and his poems, popular for many years, have been called both ascetic and epic. Jorge de Lima (1893–1953), who took a great interest in the cultural traditions of the black population of Brazil, published in 1952 *Invention of Orpheus (Invenção de Orfeu).* In 1953 appeared *The Romance of Non-Confidence (Romanceiro da Inconfidência)* by Cecília Meireles (1901–1964), who wrote crystalline metaphysical lyrics.

As the new generation of poets was beginning to take hold in the mid-fifties, the poetic and critical work of Mário Faustino (1930–1962) was of major importance. Benedito Nunes, in the preface to a reissue of Faustino's only published work, *Man and His Time (O Homem e Sua Hora)* (1955), calls attention to the impact of the page of poetic analysis and appreciation that the poet edited for three years (1956–1958) in the

Sunday supplement of the Rio periodical *Jornal do Brasil*. When Mário Faustino died in 1962 at the age of thirty-two in an airplane accident, he left behind him not only a mature poetry, some examples of which are presented in this anthology, but also critical work that revitalized Brazilian poetry.

The fifties and sixties in Brazil brought an economic growth of astonishing proportions and also rapid and severe changes in the government. In 1954, because of political pressure, the president-elect, Getúlio Vargas, who had controlled the country from 1930 to 1945, committed suicide. Vargas was loved by the masses for the social reforms that he had accomplished, and his death was a terrible shock to the nation. After his election as president in 1956, Juscelino Kubitschek guided Brazil through a period of intense industrialization. The turbulence and uncertainty of the early sixties ended in a military takeover in 1964. The military's initial hard line *(linha dura)* is fortunately but a painful memory now that the country has again begun to open up democratically.

This period of change and upheaval naturally had its effect on poetry. In the prose poem that opens this anthology Jorge Mautner speaks of the future of Brazil:

> It is the sensation that Brazil provokes of a constant going to be, going to happen, a mental vertigo, a drunkenness, an abyss of delights.

During the industrialization of the fifties and sixties, this future seemed already to have arrived, and it gave an impetus to an extraordinary development in poetry. The force of this development may be seen in Lindolf Bell's vision of a dream in a city of glass houses:

> And the dream? Ah, the dream!
> A cat atop the glass roofs,
> burning, languid,
> alone,
> scratched, mutilated,
> trapped,
> shattered,
>
> in the whole world
> one dream
> atop the glass roofs.

This industrialization, culminating in the inauguration in 1960 of the capital, Brasília, affected literary endeavor in unexpected ways. The marked improvement in the quality of printed books made possible the visual poems of the concrete poets, who responded to technological advance by making use of technological resources in their poetry. It is significant that the leaders of the concrete poets, the brothers Haroldo and Augusto de Campos, as well as Décio Pignatari, came from São Paulo, the most industrialized city in the country. The economic and social problems accompanying rapid industrial growth were most pronounced in northeastern Brazil, the home of Ferreira Gullar. It was there that he developed a poetry of political consciousness and social criticism that made him a literary spokesman, not just for Brazil, but for all third-world countries.

The effort of the concrete poets was the first after that of the Modernists in 1922 to attempt to break the dependence on foreign literary models and to make Brazil a leader in the international avant-garde. The movement, which had its beginnings in the journal *Noigandres* (1952), was the work of the three São Paulo poets and critics: Haroldo de Campos, Augusto de Campos, and Décio Pignatari. Haroldo de Campos and Augusto de Campos were the authors of the "pilot plan for concrete poetry" (1958). And together they embarked on an ambitious series of translations, adaptations, and interpretations, including *e. e. cummings—10 poems* (1960), *Panorama of Finnegans Wake of James Joyce* (1962), and, with Décio Pignatari, Ezra Pound's *Cantos* (1960). Translation for them meant not just a verbal rendering but an interpretation of all aspects of the text. Haroldo de Campos, the principal theorist of the movement, became a dedicated student of world literature, and translated, or collaborated on, translations from Chinese, Japanese, English, Russian, German, French, Italian, Spanish, and other languages.

Visual poetry—the poem as picture—is very old. It existed in the anagrams of monks in the Middle Ages and in the emblematic poems of the English seventeenth-century poets. In the twentieth century it was revived in the *Calligrammes* of Apollinaire and in the typographical fantasies of e. e. cummings. Concrete poetry, allied to such earlier visual efforts, manifested itself in various ways throughout the world in the fifties. But while elsewhere such work often appears heavy-handed, the concrete poetry of these Brazilian poets has an extraordinary freshness, perhaps because they come from a country where poets have always displayed remarkable verbal agility (a requirement perhaps with a language as old and at times as stilted as literary Portuguese) and a highly developed visual sense.

Humor is certainly not lacking in the poems of the Brazilian concretists, as is evident in the anti-advertisement poem of Décio Pignatari, where the words *coca-cola* are cleverly transmuted into *cloaca* (sewer), or in his substitution of the head of Christ for that of George Washington on the American one-dollar bill. It is also there in the "Viva Vaia" of Augusto de Campos, which might be translated as "Hurrah for Hissing." *Viva* means *Hurrah* and *Vaia* means *hissing* so that we have the juxtaposition of opposites rendered, as they are on the original in red and white, with supreme irony.

The Brazilian poets unquestionably took the lead in concrete poetry, and their work has influenced that of poets in many other countries. Through an exchange of letters and books with Augusto de Campos, Ian Hamilton Finlay in Scotland became interested in concrete poetry and grew to be one of its principal exponents. The irony of the movement is that while it set out to change the nature of poetry in Brazil, it ended by having perhaps a greater effect abroad. In a comment on his poem "Transient Servitude," Haroldo de Campos, paraphrasing Mallarmé, says: "In a circumstance of scarcity [referring to hunger in Brazil], the poet tries to give 'un sens plus POUR aux mots de la tribu.' A committed poetry, without giving up the devices and technical achievements of concrete poetry."

This commitment does not always come through. Concrete poetry in Brazil with its elaborate, and at times over-pedantic, theoretical apparatus seemed to move farther and farther from the people it wanted to reach. Some critics saw it as the dead end of Brazil's humanistic culture, a kind of erudite Gongorism.

While the works of the concretists are, at their best, original, witty, and intellectually rewarding, it is refreshing to turn to the more accessible and overtly committed poetry of Ferreira Gullar. His book *The Bodily Struggle (A Luta Corporal)* (1954) established him as a poet able to write about down-to-earth matters in very precise language. The rotten bananas of his powerful poem become a symbol for the "afternoon's ulcer," and the scene of poverty from which the poet cannot escape. In his *Dirty Poem (Poema Sujo),* published in 1977 while he was in exile in Buenos Aires, he constructs stone by stone his native city of São Luís. As Otto Maria Carpeaux has said, *Dirty Poem* merits being called a national poem because it brings together all the experiences, victories, defeats, and hopes in the life of the ordinary Brazilian. Ferreira Gullar returned to Brazil in 1980, and has since continued his forceful role on the poetic scene.

After the Apollonian interlude of concretism, Brazilian poetry assumes once again its Dionysian aspect in the poetry of Lindolf Bell, with which this anthology concludes. The poem, he tells us, grows where nothing else will:

> Since its destiny is to grow
> it grows from the daily ashes
> and from the filth of humanity.

It has been possible to include in this anthology only a few of the principal voices of the past thirty years. Of the generation of poets whose work begins to appear in the late sixties, we should mention Leonardo Fróes, Torquato Neto, Wally Salomão, Antônio Carlos de Brito, Leomar Fróes, Isabel Câmara, and Paulo Leminski.

Leonardo Fróes may speak for all of them when, at the end of his poem, "Letter to an Old Poet" *(Carta a um Velho Poeta),* he writes:

> One fine day we awoke, our foreheads wet with dew,
> And discovered the dust of various continents embedded in our
> worn-out shoes.
>
> Today we stand barefoot and naked before the onrushing engine.
> Only dimly aware that its beam may be approaching down the tracks
> of night.
>
> Together we are momentarily stunned,
> And, unable to deceive ourselves any longer,
> We extract from the earth beneath us this signal of hope.

The ability of contemporary Brazilian poets to come up with original and convincing signs of hope even at the most difficult times makes them a vital force on the world literary scene, as we trust the poems collected here will demonstrate.

**Emanuel Brasil**
**William Jay Smith**

JORGE MAUTNER

## Dionysus in Brazil

The future is a bird that arrives, already tired from being an airplane. It is humanity crystallized in an immortal pill. It is the future of Brazil, so talked of and so certain. It is the sensation that Brazil provokes of a constant going to be, going to happen, a mental vertigo, a drunkenness, an abyss of delights.

What Europe can possess this? What Asia? Not even Africa, with the weight of its darkness and its pharaohs behind it. We are the innocent children of old assassins and our childish murmur is the samba.

*Carnival* is our earthquake.

Dionysus was packed up in Greece and shipped here, where he married an Indian and turned into one. Dionysus had a little daughter with whom he used to stroll under the shadows of the gigantic trees of Amazonia. Collected orchids for her and sang sad songs.

Translated by **Romney Meyran**

## A Casa

Debaixo do assoalho da casa
no talco preto da terra prisioneira,
quem fala?
naquela
noite menor sob os pés da família
naquele
território sem flor
debaixo das velhas tábuas
que pisamos pisamos pisamos
quando o sol ia alto
quando o sol já morria
quando o sol já morria
e eu morria
quem fala?
quem falou falou? quem falará?
na língua de fogo azul do país debaixo da casa?
Fala talvez
ali
a moeda que uma tarde rolou (a moeda uma tarde) rolou
e se apagou naquele solo lunar
Fala
talvez um rato
que nos ouvia de sob as tábuas
e conosco aprendeu a mentir
e amar
(no nosso desamparo em São Luís do Maranhão
na Camboa
dentro do sistema solar
entre constelações que da janela víamos
num relance)
Fala
talvez o rato morto fedendo até secar
E ninguém mais?
E o verão? e as chuvas
torrenciais? e a classe
operária? as poucas
festas de aniversário
não falam?

## The House

Underneath the floor of the house
in the black talc of imprisoned earth
who speaks?
in that
lesser night under the family feet
in that
flowerless territory
under the old floorboards
where we stepped stepped stepped
when the sun was rising high
when the sun was already dying
when the sun was already dying
and I was dying
who speaks?
who spoke who spoke who'll speak
in the tongue of blue fire from the country under the house?
Perhaps the coin
speaks
which one day rolled (the coin one day) rolled
and was smothered in that lunar soil
Perhaps a rat
speaks
who heard us from under the floorboards
and with us learned to lie
and love
(in our wretchedness in São Luís do Maranhão
in the slums of Camboa
within the solar system
among constellations which we saw from the window
in a flash)
Perhaps
the dead rat speaks, reeking until it shrivels
No one else?
What about summer? and the pouring
rains? and the working
class? the infrequent
birthday parties
—aren't they speaking?

A rede suja, a bilha
na janela, o girassol
no saguão clamando contra o muro
as formigas
no cimento da cozinha
Bizuza
morta
Maria Lúcia, Adí, Papai
mortos
não falam.
Mas gira, planeta, gira
oceanos azuis da minha vida.
sonhos, amores, meus
poemas de ferro,
minha luta comum,
gira,
planeta
E sobre as tábuas
a nossa vida, os nossos móveis,
a cadeira de embalo, a mesa de jantar,
o guarda-roupa
com seu espelho onde a tarde dançava rindo
feito uma menina
E as janelas abertas
por onde o espaço como um pássaro
fugia
sobrevoava as casas e rumava
num sonho
para as cidades do Sul

The dirty hammock, the clay pot
in the window, the sunflower
crying out against the garden wall
the black ants
in the kitchen cement
Grammy
dead
Maria Lúcia, Addie, Pappy
dead
they do not speak.
But spin, planet, spin,
blue oceans of my life,
dreams, loves, my
iron poems,
my common fight,
spin,
planet
And atop the floorboards
our life, our furniture,
the rocking chair, the kitchen table,
the dresser
with its mirror where daylight danced laughing
like a little girl
And the open windows
where space like a bird
was fleeing
flying over the houses and heading
in a dream
for the cities of the South

Translated by **Richard Zenith**

## As Peras

As peras, no prato,
apodrecem.
O relógio, sôbre elas,
mede
a sua morte?
Paremos a pêndula. De-
teríamos, assim, a
morte das frutas?
          Oh as peras cansaram-se
de suas formas e de
sua doçura! As peras,
concluídas, gastam-se no
fulgor de estarem prontas
para nada.
               O relógio
não mede. Trabalha
no vazio: sua voz desliza
fora dos corpos.

Tudo é o cansaço
de si. As peras se consomem
no seu doirado
sossêgo. As flôres, no canteiro
diário, ardem,
ardem, em vermelhos e azuis. Tudo
desliza e está só.
                         O dia
comum, dia de todos, é a
distância entre as cousas.
Mas o dia do gato, o felino
e sem palavras
dia do gato que passa entre os móveis,
é passar. Não entre os móveis. Pas-
sar como eu
passo: entre nada.

O dia das peras
é o seu apodrecimento.

## The Pears

On the plate the pears
decay.
The clock above them
measures out
their death?
Let us stop the pendulum: Would
we thus postpone
the death of the fruit?
        Oh, the pears have tired
of their shape and
sweetness! The pears
have spent themselves
in the final glow of preparation
for oblivion.
                The clock
does not measure. It works
in a void: its voice glides
forth from the bodies of the fruit.

Everything tires
of itself. The pears are consumed
in their golden
repose. The flowers, in their everyday
flowerbed, burn,
burn in reds and blues. Everything
glides forth and yet remains intact.
                        The common day,
everybody's day, is
the distance between things.
But the day of the cat, the feline
wordless day, that moves through the furniture
moves just to move on. Not through the furniture. But to
move on as I
move on: through the void.

The day of the pears
is its decay.

É tranquilo o dia
das peras? Elas
não gritam, como
o galo.

Gritar
para quê? se o canto
é apenas um arco
efêmero fora do
coração?

Era preciso que
o canto não cessasse
nunca. Não pelo
canto (canto que os
homens ouvem) mas
porque, can-
tando, o galo
é sem morte.

Is it tranquil
the day of the pears? They do not
cry like the cock.

Why
cry—when their song
is but an ephemeral
curve out of the heart?

Their singing must never
stop. Not because
their singing is the singing
men hear but
because, sing-
ing, the cock
knows no death.

Translated by **William Jay Smith**

## Coisas da Terra

Todas as coisas de que falo estão na cidade
    entre o céu e a terra.
São todas elas coisas perecíveis
    e eternas como o teu riso
    a palavra solidária
    minha mão aberta
ou este esquecido cheiro de cabelo
    que volta
    e acende sua flama inesperada
no coração de maio.

Todas as coisas de que falo são de carne
    como o verão e o salário.
Mortalmente inseridas no tempo,
estão dispersas como o ar
no mercado, nas oficinas,
nas ruas, nos hotéis de viagem.

    São coisas, todas elas,
    cotidianas, como bocas
    e mãos, sonhos, greves,
    denúncias,
acidentes do trabalho e do amor. Coisas,
    de que falam os jornais
    às vezes tão rudes
    às vezes tão escuras
que mesmo a poesia as ilumina com dificuldade.

    Mas é nelas que te vejo pulsando,
    mundo novo,
ainda em estado de soluços e esperança.

## Things of the Earth

All the things I speak of lie in the city
        between heaven and earth.
All are things perishable
        and eternal like your laughter
        words of allegiance
        my open hand
or the forgotten smell of hair
        that returns
        and kindles a sudden flame
in the heart of May.

All the things I speak of are of the flesh
        like summer and salary.
Mortally inserted into time
dispersed like air
in the marketplace, in offices,
streets and hostelries.

        They are things, all of them,
        quotidian things, like mouths
        and hands, dreams, strikes,
        denunciations—
accidents of work or love. Things
        talked about in the newspapers
        at times so crude
        at times so dark
that even poetry illuminates them with difficulty.

        But in them I see you, new world,
        pulsating,
still sobbing, still hopeful.

Translated by **William Jay Smith**

## Agosto 1964

Entre lojas de flores e de sapatos, bares,
	mercados, butiques,
viajo
	num ônibus Estrada de Ferro-Leblon.
	Volto do trabalho, a noite em meio,
	fatigado de mentiras.

O ônibus sacoleja. Adeus, Rimbaud,
relógio de lilazes, concretismo,
neoconcretismo, ficções da juventude, adeus,
	que a vida
	eu a compro à vista aos donos do mundo.
	Ao peso dos impostos, o verso sufoca,
a poesia agora responde a inquérito policial-militar.

	Digo adeus à ilusão
mas não ao mundo. Mas não à vida,
meu reduto e meu reino.
	Do salário injusto,
	da punição injusta,
	da humilhação, da tortura,
	do terror,
retiramos algo e com ele construimos um artefato

um poema
uma bandeira

## August 1964

Past flowershops and shoestores, bars,
    markets, boutiques,
I ride
    in a Ferro-Leblon bus.
    I'm returning from work, late at night,
    tired of lies.

The bus jerks forward. Farewell, Rimbaud,
lilac clock, concretism,
neoconcretism, fictions of youth, farewell,
    for I must pay cash
    to buy life from the world's proprietors.
    Verse is suffocating under the weight of taxes,
and poetry is subjected to a secret-police inquiry.

    I say farewell to illusion
but not to the world, not to life,
my redoubt and my kingdom.
    From unjust wages,
    from unjust punishment,
    from humiliation, from torture,
    from terror,
we take something and from it construct an artifact

a poem
a banner

Translated by **William Jay Smith**

## Oswald Morto

Enterrararam ontem em São Paulo
um anjo antropófago
de asas de folha de bananeira
(mais um nome que se mistura à nossa vegetação tropical)

As escolas e as usinas paulistas
não se detiveram
para olhar o corpo do poeta que anunciara a civilização do ócio

Quanto mais pressa mais vagar

O lenço em que pela última vez
assoou o nariz
era uma bandeira nacional

NOTA:
*Fez sol o dia inteiro em Ipanema*
*Oswald de Andrade ajudou o crepúsculo*
*hoje domingo 24 de outubro de 1954*

## Oswald Dead

Yesterday in São Paulo they buried
an anthropophagic angel
with wings made of banana leaves
(one more name to encroach on our tropical vegetation)

The schools and mills of São Paulo
didn't take time
to look at the body of the poet who prophesied the leisure civilization

The faster you go the idler you get

The handkerchief with which for the last time
he wiped his nose
was a national flag

NOTE:
*It was a sunny day in Ipanema*
*Oswald de Andrade helped the sun set*
*today Sunday, October 24, 1954*

Translated by **Richard Zenith**

## Bananas Podres

Como um relógio de ouro o podre
oculto nas frutas
sobre o balcão (ainda mel
dentro da casca
na carne que se faz água) era
ainda ouro
o turvo açúcar
vindo do chão
                    e agora
ali: bananas negras
                    como bolsas moles
                    onde pousa uma abelha
                    e gira
                    e gira ponteiro no universo dourado
                    (parte mínima da tarde)
em abril
          enquanto vivemos.

## Rotten Bananas

Like a gold watch the blight
hidden in the fruits
on the counter (still honey
under the skin
in the pulp which will turn to water) was
still golden
muddy sugar
from the ground
                              and now
look: black bananas
                              like soft bags
                              where a bee hovers
                              and spins
                              a watch hand spinning in the golden universe
                              (early afternoon)
in April
          while we live our lives.

E detrás da cidade
(das pessoas na sala
ou costurando)
às costas das pessoas
à frente delas
à direita ou
(detrás das palmas dos coqueiros
alegres
e do vento)
feito um cinturão azul
e ardente
o mar
batendo o seu tambor

que
da quitanda
não se escuta

And behind the city
(of people sitting
or sewing)
in back of the people
in front of them
to the right or
(behind the happy coconut tree
leaves
and the wind)
like a blue burning
belt
the sea
beating its drum

which
can't be heard
from the fruit stand

Que tem a ver o mar
com estas bananas
                    já manchadas de morte?
que ao nosso
lado viajam
para o caos
          e azedando
e ardendo em água e ácidos
a caminho da noite
vertiginosamente devagar?

Que tem a ver o mar
com esse marulho
de águas sujas
fervendo nas bananas?
com estas vozes que falam de vizinhos,
de bundas, de cachaça?

Que tem a ver o mar com esse barulho?

What does the sea have to do
with these bananas
already splotched with death?
which travel
with us
to chaos
souring
and burning in water and acids
on the night road
in slow vertigo?

What does the sea have to do
with those raging
dirty waters
seething in the bananas?
with these voices that talk about neighbors,
fat asses, and booze?

What does the sea have to do with that racket?

Que tem a ver o mar com este quintal?

Aqui, de azul,
apenas há um caco
de vidro de leite de magnésia
(osso de anjo)
que se perderá na terra fofa
conforme à ação giratória da noite
e dos perfumes nas folhas
do hortelã
                    Nenhum alarde
nenhum alarme
mesmo quando o verão passa gritando
sobre os nossos telhados

What does the sea have to do with this backyard?

Here there
is just a broken blue piece
from a milk of magnesia bottle
(angel bone)
that will be lost in the gentle earth
under the spinning spell of the night
and the perfumes
in the mint leaves
                                        No notice
no alarm
even when summer passes
over our roofs
screaming

Pouco tem a ver o mar
com este banheiro de cimento
e zinco
onde o silêncio é água:
uma esmeralda
engastada no tanque
(e que
solta
se esvai pelos esgotos
por baixo da cidade)

Em tudo aqui há mais passado que futuro
mais morte do que festa:
neste
banheiro
de água salobra e sombra
muito mais que de mar
há de floresta

The sea has little to do
with this cement and zinc
bathroom
where silence is water:
an emerald
inlaid in the washtub
(and which
loosened
will disappear into the sewers
underneath the city)

In all this there is more past than future
more death than mirth:
in this
dark bathroom
with its brackish water
there is much more of the forest
than of the sea

Muito mais que de mar
neste banheiro
há de bananas podres na quitanda

e nem tanto pela água
em que se puem (onde
um fogo ao revés
foge no açúcar)
do que pelo macio dessa vida
de fruta
inserida na vida da família:
um macio de banho às três da tarde.

There is much more of the rotten fruit-stand bananas
than of the sea
in this bathroom

resulting not so much from the water
in which they decay (where
a reverse fire
burns in the sugar)
as from that gentle fruit
life installed in the life of the family:
a gentle bath at three p.m.

Um macio de casa no Nordeste
com seus quartos e sala
seu banheiro
que esta tarde atravessa para sempre

Um macio de luz ferindo a vida
no corpo das pessoas
lá no fundo

onde bananas podres mar azul
fome tanque floresta
são um mesmo estampido
um mesmo grito

A gentle house in the Northeast
with its bedrooms and living room
its bathroom
which this afternoon traverses forever

A gentle light piercing the life
in a person's body
deep down

where rotten bananas blue sea
hunger washtub forest
are all one shot
one shout

E as pessoas conversam
na cozinha
ou na sala contam casos
e na fala que falam
(esse barulho)
tanto marulha o mar quanto a floresta
tanto
fulgura o mel da tarde
—o podre fogo—
                    como fulge
a esmeralda de água
                    que se foi

And the people talk
in the kitchen
or tell stories in the living room
and in the speech spoken
(that racket)
the sea rages as much as the forest
the honey of the afternoon
—the blighting fire—
                                        glistens as much as
the emerald of water
                                        that disappeared

Só tem que ver o mar com seu marulho?
com seus martelos brancos
seu diurno
relâmpago
que nos cinge a cintura?

Does the sea have to do only with its raging?
with its white hammers
its diurnal
lightning flash
that girds our waist?

O mar
        só tem a ver o mar com este banheiro
com este verde quintal com esta quitanda
        só tem a ver
        o mar
com esta noturna
terra de quintal
onde gravitam perfumes e futuros
        o mar o mar
com seus pistões azuis com sua festa
        tem a ver tem a ver
com estas bananas
        onde a tarde apodrece feito uma
carniça vegetal que atrai abelhas
varejeiras
        tem a ver com esta gente com estes homens
que o trazem no corpo e até no nome
        tem a ver com estes cômodos escuros
com estes móveis queimados de pobreza
com estas paredes velhas com esta pouca
vida que na boca
é riso e na barriga
é fome

The sea
the sea has to do only with this bathroom
with this green yard with this fruit stand
the sea
has to do only
with this nocturnal
backyard earth
where perfumes and futures gravitate
the sea the sea
with its blue pistons with its rejoicing
has to do has to do
with these bananas
where the afternoon rots like a
vegetarian slaughter attracting
blowflies
has to do with these people with these men
who carry it in their bodies and even in their names
has to do with these lightless rooms
with this furniture burned by poverty
with these old walls with this meager
life: a laugh in the mouth
and in the stomach
hunger

No fundo da quitanda
na penumbra
                    ferve a chaga da tarde
e suas moscas:
em torno dessa chaga está a casa
e seus fregueses

o bairro
as avenidas
as ruas os quintais outras quitandas
outras casas com suas cristaleiras
outras praças ladeiras e mirantes
donde se vê o mar
nosso horizonte

Rio, novembro 1978

In the back of the fruit stand
in the shadows
                    the afternoon's ulcer seethes
with its flies:
surrounding this sore are the store
and its customers

the neighborhood
the boulevards
the streets the yards other fruit stands
other houses with their china cupboards
other sloping plazas and belvederes
from which you can see the sea
our horizon

Translated by **Richard Zenith**

## Um Sorriso

Quando
com minhas mãos de labareda
te acendo e em rosa
embaixo
te espetalas

quando
com meu aceso archote e cego
penetro a noite de tua flor que exala
urina
e mel—
que busco eu com toda essa assassina
fúria de macho?
que busco eu
em fogo
aqui embaixo?
senão colher com a repentina
mão do delírio
uma outra flor: a do sorriso
que no alto o teu rosto ilumina?

## A Smile

When I
with my hands afire
ignite you and below
                    into a rose
                    you open

when I
        with my torch burning and blind
penetrate the night of your flower exhaling
urine
and nectar—
                    what am I after with this killing
masculine rage?
                        what am I seeking
                                                in the fire
                        here below,
                        if not to pluck with the abrupt
                        hand of delirium
                        another flower: the smile
                        higher up
                        that makes your face shine?

Translated by **Richard Zenith**

## Subversiva

A poesia
quando chega
não respeita nada.
Nem pai nem mãe.
Quando ela chega
de qualquer de seus abismos
desconhece o Estado e a Sociedade Civil
desrespeita o Código de Águas
relincha
como puta
nova
em frente ao Palácio da Alvorada.

E só depois
reconsidera: beija
nos olhos os que ganham mal
embala no colo
os que têm sede de felicidade
e de justiça

E promete incendiar o país

## Subversive

Poetry
when she comes
respects nothing.
Neither father nor mother.
When she struggles
up from one of her abysses
she ignores Society and the State
disdains Water Regulations
hee-haws
like a young
whore
in front of the Palace of Dawn.*

And only later
does she reconsider: kisses
the eyes of those who earn little
gathers into her arms
those who thirst for happiness
and justice

And promises to set the country on fire.

Translated by **William Jay Smith**

*The presidential palace in Brasília. —Tr.

## Homem Sentado

Neste divã recostado
à tarde
num canto do sistema solar
em Buenos Aires
(os intestinos dobrados
dentro da barriga, as pernas
sob o corpo)
                    vejo pelo janelão da sala
parte da cidade:
                          estou aqui
apoiado apenas *em mim mesmo*
neste meu corpo magro, mistura
de nervos e ossos
vivendo
à temperatura de 36 graus e meio
lembrando plantas verdes
que já morreram

## Man Seated

Leaning back on this sofa
in the afternoon
in a corner of the solar system
in Buenos Aires
(intestines doubled up
inside my belly, legs
below my body)
                    through the living-room window
I see part of the city:
                         here I am
hardly supported *by myself*
by this thin body of mine, a mixture
of nerves and bones
living
at 98.6 degrees Fahrenheit
remembering green plants
that have died.

Translated by **William Jay Smith**

## Servidão de passagem

### Proem

môsca ouro?
môsca fôsca.

môsca prata?
môsca preta.

môsca íris?
môsca reles.

môsca anil?
môsca vil.

môsca azul?
môsca môsca.

môsca branca?
poesia pouca.

*

o azul é puro?
o azul é pus

de barriga vazia

o verde é vivo?
o verde é virus

de barriga vazia

o amarelo é belo
o amarelo é bile

de barriga vazia

o vermelho é fúcsia?
o vermelho é fúria

de barriga vazia

a poesia é pura?
a poesia é para

de barriga vazia

## Transient Servitude

### Proem

fly of gold?
fly gone dry.

fly of silver?
fly of cinders.

fly of rainbows?
fly of rags.

fly of indigo?
fly of indigence.

fly of blue?
fly of flies.

fly of white?
poetry no-poetry.

*

blue's pure?
blue's pus

to empty belly

green's vivid?
green's virus

to empty belly

yellow's vaunted?
yellow's vomit

to empty belly

red's fuchsia?
red's frenzy

to empty belly

poetry's pure?
poetry's purpose

to empty belly

*

poesia em tempo de fome
fome em tempo de poesia

poesia em lugar do homem
pronome em lugar do nome

homem em lugar de poesia
nome em lugar do pronome

poesia de dar o nome

nomear é dar o nome

nomeio o nome
nomeio o homem
no meio a fome

nomeio a fome

*

poetry in time of hunger
hunger in time of poetry

poetry in place of humanity
pronoun in place of noun

humanity in place of poetry
noun in place of pronoun

poetry of giving the name

naming is giving the noun

i name the noun
i name humanity
in mid-naming is hunger

i name it hunger

## Poem

de sol a sol
soldado
de sal a sal
salgado
de sova a sova
sovado
de suco a suco
sugado
de sono a sono
sonado

sangrado
de sangue a sangue

from sun to solar
solder
from salt to salty
saline
from stick to stone
stunned
from sap to sugar
sucked
from sleep to slip
slumped

sanguined
from seep to spurt

*

onde mói esta moagem
onde engrena esta engrenagem

moenda homem moagem
moagem homem moenda

*

where does this grinding grind
where does this gear engage

grindstone man's grinding
grinding man's grindstone

engrenagem
gangrenagem

*

de lucro a lucro
logrado
de lôgro a lôgro
lucrado
de lado a lado
lanhado
de lôdo a lôdo
largado

*

sol a sal
sal a sova
sova a suco
suco a sono
sono a sangue

*

onde homem
essa moagem
onde carne
essa carnagem
onde osso
essa engrenagem

*

homem forrado
homem forrado

homem rapina
homem rapado

homem surra
homem surrado

homem buraco
homem burra

gearchanged
gangrengaged

*

from profit to profit
pinched
from pinch to pinch
profited
from pole to pole
parted
from puddle to puddle
poleaxed

*

sun to salt
salt to stun
stun to sap
sap to sleeping
sleeping to bleeding

*

with man
this bonegrind
with flesh
this bloodgut
with bone
this baregear

*

bland man
branded man

pillage man
peeled man

cudgel man
cudgelled man

sieve man
steel-safe man

*

homem senhor
homem servo

homem sôbre
homem sob

homem saciado
homem saqueado

homem servido
homem sôrvo

*

homem come
homem fome

homem fala
homem cala

homem sôco
homem saco

homem mó
homem pó

*

quem baraço
quem vassalo

quem cavalo
quem cavalga

quem explora
quem espólio

*

quem carrasco
quem carcassa

quem usura
quem usado

*

sir man
serving man

super man
sub man

stacked man
sacked man

served man
swallowed man

*

trencher man
empty man

yakkity man
rabbity man

socko man
sick man

graft man
chaff man

*

who's lord
who's lout

who's the horse
who's on horseback

who's the exploiter
who's the spoil

*

who's hangman
who's hanged man

who's usury
who's used

quem pilhado
quem pilhagem

*

quem uisque
quem urina
quem feriado
quem faxina
quem volúpia
quem vermina

*

carne carniça carnagem

sangragem sangria sangue

*

homemmoendahomemmoagem

*

açúar
nesse bagaço?

almíscar
nesse sovaco?

petunia
nesse melaço?

*

indigo nesse buraco?

*

ocre
acre
osga
asco

who's plundered
who's plundering

*

who's whisky
who's piss
who's feast-day
who's fatigue-duty
who's lust
who's lice

*

flesh filth fury

bloodbath bleeding blood

*

grindstonemangrindingman

*

sugar
in these husks?

musk
in this armpit?

petunia
in these molasses?

*

indigo in this snakepit?

*

ochre
acrid
lizard
lazar

*

canga cangalho cagaço
cansaço cachaço canga
carcassa cachaça gana

*

de mingua a mingua
de magro a magro
de morgue a morgue
de morte a morte

*

só moagem
ossomoagem
sem miragem
selvaselvagem

*

servidão de passagem

*

halter harness hot-seat
heaviness head-hot halter
hangdog half-tot anger

*

from dearth to dearth
from drouth to drouth
from deadhouse to deadhouse
from death to death

*

lonely grindinghood
bone-grindinghood
no mirage to brood
through savage wood

*

transient servitude

Translated by **Edwin Morgan**

## NOTE

The book **transient servitude** is composed of two parts: *"Proem"* and *"Poem." Proem* contains three pieces, which develop, in a dialectical way, the linguistic and existential play between *poesia pura* (pure poetry) and *poesia para* (committed poetry, poetry with a social purpose, poetry *for*). The first one is the fly of blue; the second, the fly of flies. Hölderlin: *"Und wozu Dichter in dürftiger Zeit?"* (And what is poetry for in a time of scarcity?). And Heidigger about Hölderlin: "Poetry is the foundation of *being* through the word." These somewhat metaphysical statements are transformed by the poem into a physical matter of facts: hunger in Brazilian underdeveloped regions, as a counterweight in the poet's mind, in the very act of compounding his poem: *nomeio o nome* (I name the noun), *nomeio o homem* (I name humanity), *no meio a fome* (in mid-naming is hunger); in Portuguese, by the mere cutting of the word *nomeio* is obtained non-discursively *no meio* (in the middle) which introduces "hunger" in the very act of nominating. Feuerbach: *"Der Mensch ist was er isst"* (Man is what he eats) and Brecht: *"Erst kommt das Fressen denn kommt die Moral"* (First comes grub, then comes the moral). In a circumstance of scarcity, the poet tries to give *"un sens plus* POUR *aux mots de la tribu."* A committed poetry, without giving up the devices and technical achievements of concrete poetry.

—**Haroldo de Campos**
Translated by Edwin Morgan

# esboços para uma nékuia

## SKETCHES FOR A NEKUIA

# νέκυια

o caos facetado

desço

até

tocar no

negros revérberos no negro luz negra pólem no escuro

nigromante isto

mão de baralho espadas

NÉKUIA

os sem-narinas

o olho da mosca

estojo de chumbo

fundo

asfódelos à beira-Letes

inscrito no código nucleico

uma

cartas marcadas

vozes

farejando o fosso

dois corpos

estátua áurea

degolada

nos lençóis

se encorpam

o

o AMOR

crisálidas ar

ex pulsam

crisólitos

jorro! chuva de ouro

ENSOLARA

num

CORPO

canibal um foco de vermelhos

BRANCO

o
lótus
estala
no
ócciput

ABSOLUTO

últimas

o alfabeto
das
vértebras

pétalas

lapso luciferário

ente

ENTENEBRECE

graias trés

nebrece

chumbo

gralhas grisalhas

o peso da descida

o amor e seu abutre    o amor

entenebrece

de bile quando sede

o fundo

fundo

SOL roxo índigo

túnel cadaveroso

os sem-narinas

tuberas

papáveros

flora de cavernas

putresco

piso de papoulas

onde é carnívoras

descida

farejam rostos farináceos

um fio potável é ali

mas a ira azul

das moscas

varejeiras

coagula putresco

signos tempestuosos

e assignam i punti

sousândrade

os andes sol

momentos-íris

oswald

os dentes

caninos

HÚBRIS

folguedos de tigre

afastam do fosso                                        os sem-narinas

sanha diamantina

topázio colérico

kilkerry

traquéia dessangrada

fragmentos   estes

luminosi

do CAOS

da crisálida a

LAPSO

o COSMO

borboleta-dragão um leque íris

de alas fremente

ventarola

por um minuto

pleniluz

leque fechado

pó de letras no vento

un ritmo os casos

do acaso

este poema

pende

aceso friso de

gerânios

ocaso

como um

faceted chaos eye of fly
I descend lead casing
until
I touch the depths

black reflected in black black light pollen in the dark asphodels by Lethe-side
necromancer this inscribed in the nucleic code
dealt hand spades one
marked cards

NEKUIA voices
the noseless sniffing the pit

LOVE

two bodies

chrysalises air

gilded statue

ex pulsing

beheaded

in the sheets

chrysolites

spurt! golden rain

SUNFILLS

embodied

in a

the

cannibal

BODY focus of reds

the
lotus
explodes
in the occiput

BLANK

ABSOLUTE last

(alphabet
of the
vertebrae)

petals

luciferous lapse

being

BEDIMS

harpies three

dims
lead

burden of descent

bedims

the deep
depths

hoary harpies

love and its vulture

with bile when thirsty

love

SUN purple        indigo                                        I putrefy

cadaverous tunnel                                        ground of carnivorous
                                                                  poppies where is

                                                                  descent

the noseless        sniff        furfural faces

a potable trickle        is there

but the fury        blue
of blow-
flies

tuberous roots
papaveraceous juice
cavern flora

coagulates        I putrefy

tempestuous signs

they assign i punti

sousândrade
the andes sun
rainbow moments

oswald

canine
teeth

HYBRIS
tiger frolics
rout from the pit the noseless

diamond rage

wrathful topaz

kilberry

blood-drained trachea

fragments these
luminosi

from CHAOS the COSMOS

from chrysalis to dragon-butterfly a rainbow fan
of wings quivering
crescent

for a minute

plenilight

LAPSE

closed fan

dust of lettering on the wind

a rhythm the happenings of happenstance this poem

hangs

ignited frieze of

geraniums

happenchance

like a

Translated by **Jean R. Longland**

## NOTES

NEKUIA: sacrifice for the dead (Greek); cf. *Odyssey,* Canto XI; Ezra Pound, *The Cantos,* I.

Sousândrade: Joaquim de Sousa Andrade (1832–1902). The "accursed" poet of Brazilian romanticism, author of a long epic-dramatic poem *O Guesa* (definitive edition, 1888). The poet sings the Utopian social revolution, modeled on the communal organization of the Incas, opposing paradisiacal moments ("rainbow-moments") to passages of inferno ("O Tatuturema"; "The Inferno of Wall Street") in the course of his long poem.

Kilkerry: Pedro Kilkerry (1885–1917), symbolist poet from Bahia, of the lineage of Mallarmé. He died at thirty-two of a tracheotomy. His work was rescued from oblivion and published by Augusto de Campos.

Oswald de Andrade: (1890–1953). The most radical of the Brazilian modernists, leader of the "Anthropophagous" movement, whose manifesto dates from 1928. The Brazilian concrete poets claimed him as patron of the new vanguard in their "pilot plan" of 1958. Sousândrade, Kilkerry, and Oswald are invoked as "tempestuous signs," able to rout the mediocrity of the "noseless" and permit the new erruption of poetic HYBRIS (pride, creative insolence), whose result is the gift of the poem ("cosmos" ransomed by an instant of "chaos"—"frieze of geraniums"... suspended... "like a rhythm"). NEKUIA is a descent to the infernos of memory, in order to reverence and auscultate the dead who remain alive ("tempestuous signs") through the germinative force of their poetic lesson, and to rout the "noseless"—"the dead dead" of the commonplace present. As in Sousândrade, the author opposes moments of infernal descent to paradisiacal moments of ecstatic epiphany. However, he allows those moments to interpenetrate in rapid counterpoint, by means of a syntax stripped of connectives, which tends to parataxis. The reader is invited to reconstruct the stages of the descent and the pulsations of the "rainbow-moments" as in a mental theater, "tiger frolics."

—**Haroldo de Campos**
Translated by **Jean R. Longland**

## Prefácio

Quem fez esta manhã, quem penetrou
À noite os labirintos do tesouro,
Quem fez esta manhã predestinou
Seus temas a paráfrases do touro,
A traduções do cisne: fè-la para
Abandonar-se a mitos essenciais,
Desflorada por impetos de rara
Metamorfose alada, onde jamais
Se exaure o deus que muda, que transvive.
Quem fez esta manhã fè-la por ser
Um raio a fecundá-la, não por lívida
Ausência sem pecado e fè-la ter
Em si principio e fim: ter entre aurora
E meio-dia um homem e sua hora.

## Preface

Who made this morning, who fathomed
The labyrinths of treasure in the night,
Who made this morning predestined
Its text to paraphrases of Taurus
And translations of Cygnus: made it
To be consumed by vital myths,
Deflowered by impulses of a rare
Winged metamorphosis in which the god,
Changing, and living transformed, never tires.
Who made this morning made it so as to be
A ray that could penetrate it, not a pale
Sinless absence, and made it with
Beginning and end in itself: between daybreak
And noon a man and his hour.

Translated by **Richard Zenith**

## Sinto Que o Mês Presente Me Assassina

Sinto que o mês presente me assassina,
As aves atuais nasceram mudas
E o tempo na verdade tem domínio
Sobre homens nus ao sul de luas curvas.
Sinto que o mês presente me assassina,
Corro despido atrás de um cristo preso,
Cavalheiro gentil que me abomina
E atrai-me ao despudor da luz esquerda
Ao beco de agonia onde me espreita
A morte espacial que me ilumina.
Sinto que o mês presente me assassina
E o temporal ladrão rouba-me as fêmeas
De apóstolos marujos que me arrastam
Ao longo da corrente onde blasfemas
Gaivotas provam peixes de milagre.
Sinto que o mês presente me assassina,
Há luto nas rosáceas desta aurora,
Há sinos de ironia em cada hora
(Na libra escorpiões pesam-me a sina)
Há panos de imprimir a dura face
À fôrça de suor, de sangue e chaga.
Sinto que o mês presente me assassina,
Os derradeiros astros nascem tortos
E o tempo na verdade tem domínio
Sobre o morto que enterra os próprios mortos.
O tempo na verdade tem domínio,
Amen, amen vos digo, tem domínio
E ri do que desfere verbos, dardos
De falso eterno que retornam para
Assassinar-nos num mês assassino.

## This Month Will Kill Me I Feel It

This month will kill me I feel it,
Today's birds were born mute
And time is truly sovereign
Over naked men south of curved moons.
This month will kill me I feel it,
I run unclothed behind a captive christ,
A noble gentleman who loathes me
And lures me to the gall of the crooked light
In the alley of agony where I am watched
By the spatial death that illumines me.
This month will kill me I feel it
And the thieving tempest takes from me the dames
Of sailor apostles who drag me
Along the current where irreverent
Seagulls sample miracled fish.
This month will kill me I feel it,
The roses of this dawn are mourning,
Bells ring irony on the hour
(Libra's scorpions weigh out my fate),
There are cloths for imprinting the hard face
By force of sweat, of blood and festering flesh.
This month will kill me I feel it,
The lastborn stars are deformed
And time is truly sovereign
Over the dead who bury their own dead.
Time is truly sovereign,
Amen, Amen I say to thee, is sovereign
And laughs at who hurls words, eternally
False darts that return to
Kill us in a killing month.

Translated by **Richard Zenith**

## Vida Toda Linguagem

Vida toda linguagem,
frase perfeita sempre, talvez verso,
geralmente sem qualquer adjetivo,
coluna sem ornamento, geralmente partida.
Vida toda linguagem,
há entretanto um verbo, um verbo sempre, e um nome
aqui, ali, assegurando a perfeição
eterna do período, talvez verso,
talvez interjetivo, verso, verso.
Vida toda linguagem,
feto sugando em língua compassiva
o sangue que criança espalhará—oh metáfora ativa!
leite jorrado em fonte adolescente,
sêmen de homens maduros, verbo, verbo.
Vida toda linguagem,
bem o conhecem velhos que repetem,
contra negras janelas, cintilantes imagens
que lhes estrelam turvas trajetórias.
Vida toda linguagem—
como todos sabemos
conjugar esses verbos, nomear
esses nomes:
amar, fazer, destruir,
homem, mulher e bêsta, diabo e anjo
e deus talvez, e nada.
Vida toda linguagem,
vida sempre perfeita,
imperfeitos sòmente os vocábulos mortos
com que um homem jovem, nos terraços do inverno, contra a chuva,
tenta fazê-la eterna—como se lhe faltasse
outra, imortal sintaxe
à vida que é perfeita
língua
eterna.

## Life Nothing but Language

Life nothing but language,
an always perfect phrase, perhaps verse,
generally without any adjectives,
an unornamented column, generally split.
Life nothing but language,
but there is a word, always a word, and a name
here, there, insuring the eternal
perfection of the period, perhaps verse,
perhaps interjection, verse, verse.
Life nothing but language,
fetus sucking up with compassionate tongue
the blood which child will splatter—oh busy metaphor!
milk spurting in adolescent spring,
semen of mature men, word, word.
Life nothing but language,
as the old ones know, who repeat,
against black windows, scintillating images
that spangle their overcast trajectories.
Life nothing but language—
                                        we all know how
to conjugate those verbs, name
those names:
                    to love, to make, to destroy,
man, woman and beast, devil and angel
and god perhaps, and nothing.
Life nothing but language,
life always perfect,
only the dead words imperfect,
words with which a young man, in winter's terraces, against the rain,
tries to make it eternal—as if he were missing
another, immortal syntax
for the life that is perfect
                                    eternal
                                            language.

Translated by **Richard Zenith**

## Juventude—

. . .

Juventude—
a jusante a maré entrega tudo—

maravilha do vento soprando sobre a maravilha
de estar vivo e capaz de sentir
maravilhas no vento—
amar a ilha, amar o vento, amar o sopro, o rasto—
maravilha de estar ensimesmado
(a maravilha: vivo!),
tragado pelo vento, assinalado
nos pélagos do vento, recomposto
nos pósteros do tempo, assassinado
na pletora do vento—
maravilha de ser capaz,
maravilha de estar a postos,
maravilha de em paz sentir
maravilhas no vento
e apascentar o vento,
encapelado vento—
mar à vista da ilha,
eternidade à vista
do tempo—
o tempo: sempre o sopro
etéreo sobre os pagos, sobre as régias do vento,
do montuoso vento—
e a terna idade amarga—juventude—
êxtase ao vivo, ergue-se o vento lívido,
vento salgado, paz de sentinela
maravilhada à vista
de si mesma nas algas
do tumultuoso vento,

## Youth—

. . .

Youth—
downstream the tide relinquishes everything—

wonder of the wind blowing about the wonder
of being alive and able to feel
wonders in the wind—
loving the island, loving the wind, loving the breeze, the vestige—
wonder of being self-absorbed
(the wonder: I live!),
swallowed up by the wind, branded
in the wind's depths, remodeled
in the coming generations, killed
in the plethora of the wind—
wonder of being capable,
wonder of being ready,
wonder of peacefully feeling
wonders in the wind
and revelling in the wind,
turbulent wind—
sea seen from the island,
eternity seen
from time—
time: always the ethereal blowing
above the birthplace, above the castles of the wind,
the mountainous wind—
and the tender bitter age—youth—
ecstasy to the living, the livid wind lifts up,
salty wind, peace standing watch
awed at the sight
of itself in the algae
of the tumultuous wind,

de seus restos na mágua
do tumulário tempo,
de seu pranto nas águas do mar justo—
maravilha de estar assimilado
pelo vento repleto
e pelo mar completo—juventude—

a montante a maré apaga tudo—

. . .

of its remains in the anguish
of entombing time,
of its weeping in the waters of the just sea—
wonder of being assimilated
by the replete wind
and by the complete sea—youth—

upstream the tide quenches everything—

. . .

Translated by **Richard Zenith**

## Cavossonante Escudo Nosso

Cavossonante escudo nosso
        palavra: panacéia
ornado de consolos e compensas
enquanto a seta-fado
nos envenena ambos tendões
                                rachados.

No sabuloso mar na salsa areia
alimento não cresce
                        cobras crescem
e nos impõe silêncio o bramir vero
do veado oceano
                        cio cio
verdade, matogrosso universal
viscosamente ouvida
                        não palavras não pa
lavras
                        e do cosmo selvagem
recém recém tombada:

**Amor**

estrela inominada pedra lava
escudo panejante panacéia
                                        (a cruz
se enfuna)
bólide trespassando chão-essência
peito-presença

**Aqui**

                        estamos.
Entre nome e fenômeno balança
nunca meu coração:
                            ferido sangra
pelo rosto do ser e por seus rins,
indiferente, he le na, às sílabas
véus teu ventre disfar-farçando:

## Our Hollow-sounding Shield

Our hollow-sounding shield
      word: panacea
adorned with consolations and compensations
while fate's arrow
poisons both our torn
                  tendons.

In the salty sand of the sea
food won't grow
                snakes grow
and we are silenced by the true howling
of the ocean stag
                  in heat heat heat
truth, universal forest
viscidly heard
                no words no wor
ds
                and from the wild wooded cosmos
lately lately toppled:

**Love**

nameless star stone lava
enclothing shield panacea
                                  (the cross
looms large)
falling star trespassing ground-essence
bosom-presence

**Here**

                                            we are.
Between name and phenomenon
my heart never oscillates:
                            wounded it bleeds
from life's face and from its kidneys,
indifferent, bar ba ra, to the syllables
veils disguis-guising your insides:

êle singra êle sangra êle roxo
...espuma...
pela forma da coisa por seu pêso
e pára de pulsar rugindo contra
o que serve de rocha e despedaça
a liberdade sétima—tocar
a liberdade oitava—penetrar
a liberdade inteira—conhecer:

### Cor Ação

o sopro do metal ressoa chama
para a luta real
(há remoinhos)
cavossonante escudo rebentamos
a fraga estilhaçamos nus sem-pele
estrelorientados rumo-nós
boiamos
ainda que parados:
mudos:
somos.

it sails it bleeds purple it
  . . . foams . . .
into the shape and weight of the thing
and pulsing no more it booms against
whatever acts like rock and shatters
the seventh liberty—touching
the eighth liberty—penetrating
the final liberty—knowing:

## Heart

the murmur of the metal resounds calls
to the true fight
  (there are whirlwinds)
we split the hollow-sounding shield
and shatter the crag naked skinless
starguided our bearings
  we float
although motionless:
  voiceless:
  we are.

Translated by **Richard Zenith**

## Moriturus Salutat

O céu azula a poça
o sol
sol amarela
                    a grama.

O homem
(Soldado,
a sorte está lançada!)
avermelhando o rio.
Centopéia,
verme pé ante pé,
avanças:
posso rir-me do gamo
correndo sem sentido pela mata?
a sanguessuga avança,
eu corro com sentido:
eu mato—
eu caio sem sentidos,
ora, morro.
O monte, o verde gaio,
passa, corrente, o gamo;
ora, eu amo

o córrego sangento (avante!) eu sinto
—o céu azula a poça, o sol
sol, amarelo ramo, soltos dados:
oh sorte de cem pés, oh quem me chama?

Soldado,
progredir rosto contra
formigas,
soldado dedicado, revólver,
formas amigas,
regredir sem sentido
(inimigos?)
a fronte contra a lama:
soldado,
                quem te ama?

## Moriturus Salutat

The sky blues the pool
the sun
sun yellows
                    the grass.

Man
(Soldier,
your number's up!)
reddens the river.
Centipede,
the footed worm,
advances:
can I laugh at the stag
running for no reason through the woods?
the leech advances,
I run for a reason:
I kill—
I fall, losing all reason,
I die.
The stag runs free
over the gay green hill;
I love.

I feel the stream bleeding (forward!)
—the sky blues the pool, the sun
sun, yellow branch, flying dice:
oh fate of one hundred feet, who calls me?

Soldier,
forward! face against
ants,
dedicated soldier, gun,
sociable ants,
retreat! for no reason
(enemies?)
face in the mud:
soldier,
            who loves you?

Cubo azul, amarelo, verde, rubro,
a morte está cansada:
formiga, sanguessuga, centopéia,
revólver contra os ossos
—não querem devolver-nos o que é nosso;
o céu, o sol, o rio, gamo e ramo,
revólver: "Aqui jaz..."

—Devolverão a paz?

Blue yellow green red cube,
death is getting tired:
ant, leech, centipede,
gun pressed against the bones
—they won't give back what is ours;
the sky, sun, river, stag and branch,
gun: "Here lies..."

—Will they give back peace?

Translated by **Richard Zenith**

## Ariazul

### Ária

em honra dum ar de colina;
                                        anno primo,
infinita sazão, janeiro fim; alhures,
longe:
          ar de colina, alguém re
spire
        êstes nomes — em honra
                                            expire:
estrada    crepúsculo    altura
                                              gume-de-fôlha-de-grama
espada serrando horizonte
                                        e serra
e verbo inscrito no aço:

### Passo

Laço    laço de corda    sino enforca
espaço
          sol pesa no pescoço

### Teantropo

constelado suicida no oceano:
                                            o ano
suscita um outro ano
                                                      ar de colina
eixo celeste                                vertebral coluna
traído pela brisa                      mastro      mestre
abandona a bandeira da balança

### Noite

— Tombada a noite, rasgado o véu, santo dos santos,
para o sopé descemos, onde nos esperava
o jogo — dados, mais dados — e zumbido no ouvido —

## Blue Aria

### Aria

in honor of the mountain air;
                                                anno primo,
infinite season, January end; elsewhere,
far away:
                mountain air, someone re
spires
          these names—in honor
                                                exhales:
highway    twilight    height
                                                grass-blade-edge
sword hewing horizon
                                    and mountain
and a word inscribed in the steel:

### Pass

Noose    noose of rope    bell hangs
space
          sun weighs on the neck

### Theanthropist

constellated suicide in the ocean:
                                                one year
breeds another
                                                            mountain air
celestial axis                                  vertebral column
betrayed by the breeze                     mast        master
abandons the flag of Libra

### Night

—The night overthrown, the veil torn, holy of holies,
we climb down to the bottom, where games
await us—dice, more dice—and buzzing in the ear—

—E do salão o deslizar se ouvia
dos carros na rodovia, como se ouve
o mar—outro, mais outro—sobre as conchas atentas—

**Peso**

fiel dum lado mais que doutra lágrima
e pouso algum de pedra onde apoiar-se.
Ar raro:
            ar de colina:

                        raro

**Ar**

raro ar feito corpo. Corpo: salto
e carne. E sal roendo músculo sagrado.
Eixo celeste vertebral coluna

**Sino**

gongo
        sinal de luz total
                        ruína

gume de caule e flor
                        espada—linha
injusta de horizonte, aço gravado:

**Tudo que Passa**

—Nada. Se passa—
                        ar de colina
                                raro

**Azul**

—And from the hall was heard the skidding
of cars on the highway, as the sea
is heard—another, still another—over the listening shells—

**Weight**

faithful on one side more than another tear
and no stone perch for support.
Rare air:
            mountain air:

                        rare

**Air**

rare air like a body. Body: leap
and flesh. And salt gnawing holy muscle.
Celestial axis vertebral column

**Bell**

gong
      traffic light all
                  ruins

stem edge and flower
                  sword—unjust
horizon line, engraved steel:

**Everything that Passes**

—Nothing. It passes—
                  mountain air
                              rare

**Blue**

Translated by **Richard Zenith**

**eixoolho**
**polofixo**
**eixoflor**
**pesofixo**
**eixosolo**
**olhofixo**

**Eixo**
**Axis**

**fixteyes**
**poleaxis**
**fixtrose**
**hungaxis**
**fixtsoil**
**eyesaxis**

*eixo* = axis
*ôlho* = eye
*polo* = pole
*fixo* = fixed
*flor* = flower
*pêso* = weight
*solo* = soil

English version by Edwin Morgan

[1957]

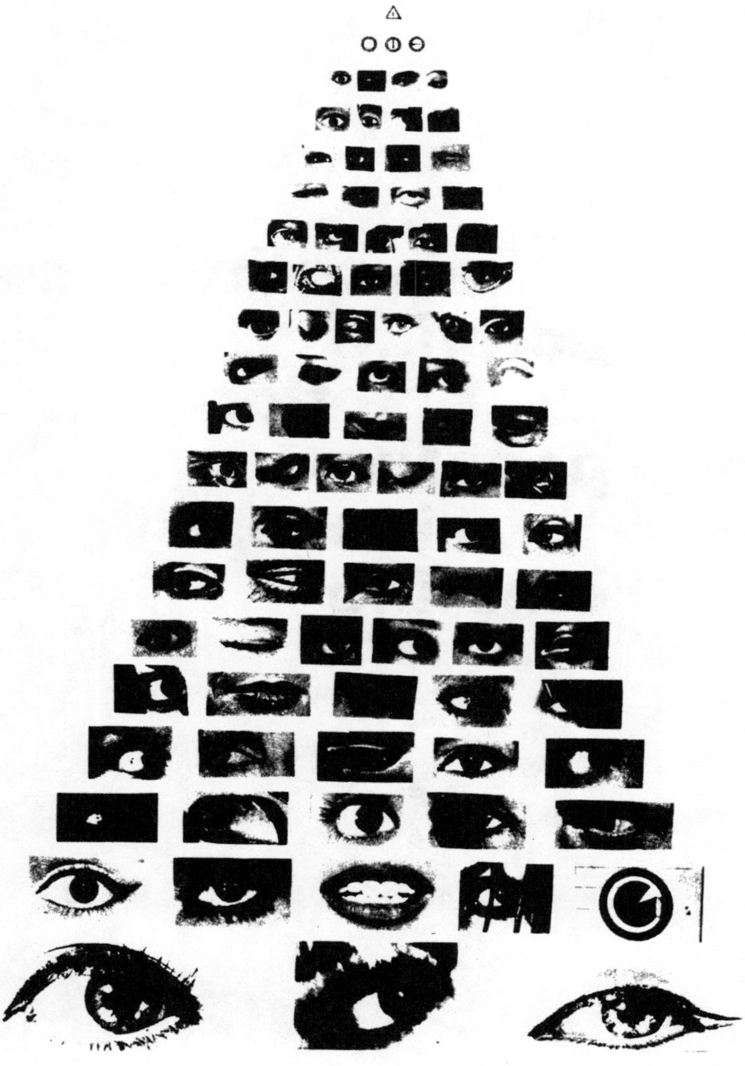

## Ôlho por Ôlho
## Eye for Eye

A Popcrete poem

**"no tongue! all eyes! be silent." [Shakespeare via Zukofsky].**

(The original is a collage in color, 50 cm. by 70 cm., composed of clippings from magazines.)

[1964]

TUDO
ESTÁ
DITO

EVERYTHING
WAS
SAID

[1974]

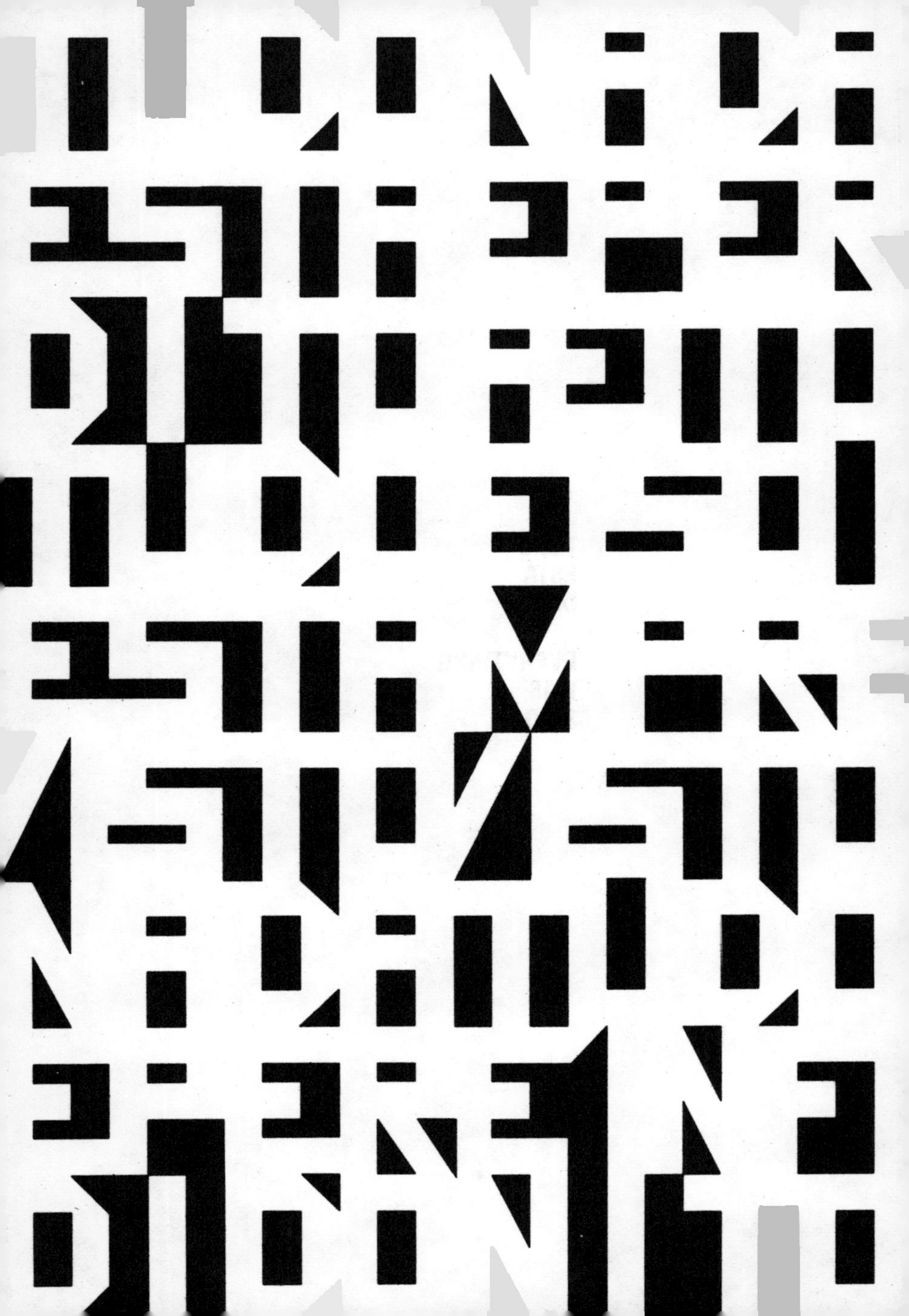

TUDO everything
ESTÁ was
DITO said

TUDO everything
ESTÁ was
VISTO seen

NADA nothing
ÉPER is lo
DIDO st

NADA nothing
ÉPER is per
FEITO fect

EIS O here is the
IMPRE unfore
VISTO seen

TUDO everything
ÉINFI is infi
NITO nite

O PULSAR

THE PULSAR

[1975]

·ND★ QU★R QU★ V·C★ ★ST★JA

★M MART★ ·U ★LD·RAD·

ABRA A JAN★LA ★ V★JA

● PULSAR QUAS★ MUD●

ABRAÇ● D★ AN●S LUZ

QU★ N★NHUM SOL AQU★C★

● OC● SCURO ·SQU·C·

ONDE QUER QUE VOCÊ ESTEJA
EM MARTE OU ELDORADO
ABRA A JANELA E VEJA
O PULSAR QUASE MUDO
ABRAÇOS DE ANOS LUZ
QUE NENHUM SOL AQUECE
E O ECO(OCO) ESCURO ESSQUECE

WHEREVER YOU ARE
IN MARS OR ELDORADO
OPEN THE WINDOW AND SEE
THE PULSAR (PULSATION) NEARLY MUTE
EMBRACE OF LIGHT YEARS
THAT NO SUN WARMS
AND THE DARK ECHO (VOID) FORGETS

## O QUASAR

## THE QUASAR

[1975]

PENSA NO QUASE AMAR DO QUASAR QUASE HUMANO

THINK OF THE QUASI-LOVE OF THE QUASI-HUMAN QUASAR

# MEMOS

MEMOS

| | | |
|---|---|---|
| COMO | AMAR | EPAS |
| PARA | GOES | SASS |
| REST | TEMO | IMPA |
| EINS | MENT | SSAA |
| TANT | OAMA | SSIM |
| ELUZ | ISQU | PASS |
| QUEA | EAME | AMEM |
| MEMO | MORI | ORIA |
| RIAA | AMOR | ASSA |
| FLOR | DEMA | SSIN |
| AMAS | SNÃO | ADOM |
| NÃOS | CONS | OMEN |
| ABER | EGUE | TOQU |
| ETER | AMAR | EPAS |

[1976]

h o w s   b i t t   p a s s
t a y t   e r t h   e s a n
h i s i   e s e m   d p a s
n s t a   a n y m   s e s a
n t l i   o m e n   n d s o
g h t w   t s w h   p a s s
h i c h   i c h m   e s m e
M E M O   E M O R   M O R Y
r y s e   y t a s   a s s a
i z e s   t e s y   s s i n
b u t f   e t c a   o f m o
a i l s   n n o t   m e n t
t o r e   e v e r   s p a s
t a i n   l o v e   s i n g

Translated by **Claus Clüver**

## A ROSE DOENTE

## THE SICK ROSE

[1975]

# A Rosa Doente

Ó Rosa, estás doente!
Um verme pela treva
Voa invisivelmente.
O vento que uiva o leva
Ao velado veludo
Do fundo do teu centro:
Seu escuro amor mudo
Te rói desde dentro.

William Blake

Illustration for "The Tiger" of Blake: From a Dervish mural, Turkey, 19th century. The letters in the body of the tiger compose a Mohammedan inscription, which means, in part: "In the name of the lion of God, of the face of God, of triumphant Ali, son of Ebu Talet." (T. K. Birge, *The Bektashi Order of Dervishes*, London, 1952, mentioned by Berjouhl Bowler in *The Word as Image*, London, Studio Vista Ltd., 1970).

# the tyger

## william blake

# o tygre

tyger ! tyger ! burning bright
in the forests of the night.
what immortal hand or eye
cd frame thy fearful symmetry ?

tygre! tygre! brilho, brasa
que 'a furna noturna abrasa,
que olho ou mào armaria
tua feroz symmetrya?

em que céu se foi forjar
o fogo do teu olhar?
em que asas veio a chamma?
que mão colheu essa flamma?

que força fez retorcer
em nervos todo o teu ser ?
e o som do teu coração
de aço, que cor, que ação ?

teu cérebro. quem o malha?
que martelo? que fornalha
o moldou? que mão. que garra
seu terror mortal amarra?

quando as lanças das estrelas
cortaram os céus. ao vê-las.
quem as fez sorriu talvez?
quem fez a ovelha te fez?

tyger: tyger: burning bright
in the forests of the night.
what immortal hand or eye
cd frame thy fearful symmetry?

tygre! tygre! brilho. brasa
que 'a furna noturna abrasa.
que olho ou mão armaria
tua feroz symmetrya?

**Pentahexagrama para John Cage**

**Pentahexagram for John Cage**

[1977]

# Noosfera

chanutes aders wrights demoiselles voisin

s blériots fluindo sedas tensas libélulas

ouro onvionleta no por de ar de ocre da t

arde lá em baixo sobre a calota megalopol

itana em olho-de-peixe sign (ÕS DECÕLANDÕ

PLANANDÕ CIRCUNVÕLUINDÕ SOBRE LÕBÕS CALÕS

QUIASMAS BULBOS VENTRICULÕS TRIGÕNÕS PEDÚ

NCULOS FENDAS DE RÕLANDÕ E SYLVIUS SÕB UM

CÉU PARIETAL)

## Noûsphere

chanutes aders wrights demoiselles blé
riots flowing taut silks dragonflies g
old onviolet in the ocher airset at du
sk down there above the megapolitan
hub in the fisheye sign (ÕS TAKING ÕFF
GLIDING CIRCUMFLYING ÕVER LÕBES CALLUS
ES QUIASMATA BULBS VENTRICULI TRIGONS
PENDUNCLES FISSURES ÕF ROLAND AND SYLV
IUS UNDER A PARIETAL SKY)

Translated by **Klaus Müller-Bergh**

beba coca cola
babe          cola
beba coca
babe cola caco
caco
cola

cloaca

***beba*** **= to drink**
***babe*** **= to slob**
***cola*** **= glue**
***caco*** **= pieces**

**An early committed concrete poem. A kind of anti-advertisement. Against the reification of the mind through slogans, demistifying of the "artificial paradise" promised by mass-persuasion techniques. *Cloaca* is made out of the same letters as Coca-Cola.**
**—Haroldo de Campos**

A cine-poem. The progression of the letters corresponds to the progression of their traces. The word is reorganized following the visual crescendo of its letters' features. With four traces we have a nucleus, where all letters are condensed and resumed. By a coincidence, this nucleus is also the Chinese ideogram for sun *(jih;* Japanese *ni),* the vital principle. After this, the nucleus explodes, producing the word LIFE. The poem develops the passage from the digital unit to the semantic corpus (word), and from the ideogram (analogical) to the phonetic word (digital), suggesting some unexpected links between both processes.

—Haroldo de Campos

# L

# F

# E

# LIFE

FEDERAL RESERVE NOTE
THE UNITED STATES OF AMERICA
THIS NOTE IS LEGAL TENDER
FOR ALL DEBTS, PUBLIC AND PRIVATE
B11359641C
B11359641C
WASHINGTON, D.C.
ONE
H3
H126
2
2
2
2
B
SERIES 1963
WASHINGTON
Treasurer of the United States.
Secretary of the Treasury.
ONE DOLLAR

**Cr$isto é a solução**

**Chr$ist is the answer**

## Poema a um Jovem

*a Jorge Mautner*

Deixem-me jogar a última jogada do Amor
que o amor da Morte me transfigura.

Deixem-me jogar o último jôgo das Trevas
que tantas trevas preciso para um instante de luz.
Oh! Como é vasta a minha pureza!
O mundo circunda-me com suas asas
e um anjo de asas maiores que o corpo
deixa a porta aberta
e o foragido
coloca a chave debaixo do tapete
com uma seta de ouro para mostrar o lugar.

Deixem-me jogar a última jogada
que eu sinto a noite como uma feira imensa.
Vou soberbo e visitante na solidão,
no empenho,
no reino de alabastros
e na praça com edifícios
sem tamanho das Trevas.

Deixem-me jogar a última jogada do Amor
nêste fastio de viver,
que êste é meu canto e meu corpo
e minha tôrre de sentinela.

## Poem to a Young Man

*To Jorge Mautner*

Let me play Love's last card
for the love of Death transfigures me.

Let me play Dark's final hand
for I need the deepest darkness to catch a flash of light.
Oh, how vast is my purity:
The world envelops me with its wings
and an angel with wings greater than its body
leaves the door open
and the fugitive
places the key under the rug
with a gold arrow indicating the spot.

Let me play the last card
for the night seems like a great fair.
A proud guest I go into solitude,
into the place of secret desire,
into the alabaster kingdom
and into the square with buildings
lacking the dimension of dark.

Weary of life,
let me play Love's last card,
for this is my niche, my body,
and my watchtower.

Translated by **William Jay Smith**

## Retrato de um Ex-jovem Burguês

Disseram-me: sorria.
E eu sorri com os dentes à mostra
como num anúncio.
E eu sorri com a bôca no espaço,
nas tardes da vida,
nas noites da vida,
nas caras da vida.
Sorria, jovem. A liberdade
abrirá as asas
com seus pêsos
e seus pêndulos.
Deixa o alicate arrancar o grito
e a revolta.
As sirenes colocarão tôdas as coisas
em ordem.
E eu sorri como um peixe
com a bôca triturada.
E eu sorri! Sorri com desespêro da hora,
da hora de sorrir.
E eu sorri por causa da obra
e da vida e da morte
e dos ramos e das ramas
e das árvores e dos rios
e de tôdas glórias
e da liberdade rameira
e de tanto sorrir
vi a vulgaridade do mundo fácil
A HUMANIDADE TEM ESCLEROSE!
Sorria, jovem, sorria,
que é próprio da juventude sorrir
e eu de tanto sorrir
aprendi a confundir as coisas e as pessoas
e a ter na infância uma boa lembrança
e a estupidez como um fruto intragável.

## Portrait of an Ex-young Bourgeois

They said to me: Smile
And I smiled with my teeth showing
as in an advertisement.
And I smiled with my mouth open onto space
onto the afternoons of life
onto the nights of life
onto the faces of life.
Smile, young man. Freedom
will open its wings
with their weights
and their pendulums.
Let the pliers extract the shout
and the revolt.
The sirens will place all things
in order.
And I smiled like a fish
with my pulverized mouth.
And I smiled! I smiled with the despair of the hour,
the hour of smiling.
And I smiled because of work
and because of life and death
and because of branches and foliage
and because of trees and rivers
and because of all the glories
and because of freedom the prostitute
and by smiling so much
I saw the vulgarity of the facile world.
HUMANITY HAS SCLEROSIS!
Smile, young man, smile,
for it is fitting for a young man to smile
and by smiling so much
I learned to confuse things and people
and to have a good memory of childhood
and of stupidity like a fruit I could not swallow.

Ah! Rebento dos deuses, rebento dos homens,
querubim de pedra de uma praça de pedra:
sorria dos anacoretas e dos bodes expiatórios
que a grande brincadeira continua.
Todos os dias são quartas-feiras de cinza.
O riso permanece numa camisa de fôrça
e o sorriso nasce do abominável.
Sorria. Deixa a náusea sobrevir
que a náusea é doce.

E eu sorrio. Sorrio dos cantos de sereia da Sociedade
e do absinto
e do incenso
e dos granizos da felicidade comum.
Sorrio do vagido torto
e imenso da vida,
dos guizos
e salamandras
e da água-lustral
e das alfaias
e das baixelas de prata
e sinto meu corpo de abcesso dilatar-se.
E então gargalho. Gargalho como um pássaro
e uma fera simples, ímpia e sem sentidos,
E ESTREMEÇO TODOS OS ALICERCES.

Ah, offshoot of the gods, offshoot of man,
stone cherub in a stone square:
smile at anchorites and scapegoats
for the great joke continues.
All days are Ash Wednesdays.
Laughter remains in a straitjacket
and the smile is born of the abominable.
Smile. Let nausea ensue
for nausea is sweet.

And I smile. I smile at the siren songs of Society
and at the absinthe
and at the incense
and at the hailstones of ordinary happiness.
I smile at the crooked and immense
wail of life,
at rattles
and salamanders
and lustral waters
and kitchen utensils
and silver services
and I feel my body swell with an abcess.
And then I guffaw. I guffaw like a bird
or a wild beast, simple, impious, and without feeling.
AND I SHAKE ALL FOUNDATIONS.

Translated by **William Jay Smith**

## O Poema das Crianças Traídas

Eu vim de geração das crianças traídas.
Eu vim de um montão de coisas destroçadas.
Eu tentei unir células e nervos mas o rebanho morreu
Eu fui à tarefa num tempo de drama.
Eu cerzi o tambor da ternura quebrado.

Eu fui às cidades destruídas para viver os soldados mortos.
Eu caminhei no caos com uma mensagem.
Eu fui lírico de granadas prêsas à respiração.
Eu visualizei as perspectivas de cada catacumba.
Eu não levei serragem aos corações dos ditadores.
Eu recolhi as lágrimas de tôdas as mães numa bacia de sombra.
Eu tive a função de porta-estandarte nas revoluções.
Eu amei uma menina virgem.

Eu arranquei das pocilgas um brado.
Eu amei os amigos de pés no chão.
Eu fui a criança sem ciranda.
Eu acreditei numa igualdade total.
Eu não fui canção mas grito de dor.
Eu tive por linguagem materna, roçar de bombas, baionetas.
Eu fechei-me numa redoma para abrir meu coração triste.
Eu fui a metamorfose de Deus.

Eu vasculhei nos lixos para redescobrir a pureza.
Eu desci ao centro da terra para colher o girassol que morava no eixo.
Eu descobri que são incontáveis os grãos no fundo do mar
[mas tão raros os que sabem o caminho da pérola.
Eu tentei persistir para além e para aquém do contexto humano,
[o que foi errado.
En procurei um avião liquidado para fazer a casa.
Eu inventei um brinquedo das molas de um tanque enferrujado.
Eu construi uma flor de arame farpado para levar na solidão.

## Poem of the Betrayed Children

I came from the generation of the betrayed children.
I came from a heap of wreckage.
I tried to unite cells and nerves but the herd died.
I took up the task in a time of tragedy.
I patched the ruptured drum of tenderness.

I went to the ruined cities to live the soldier's death.
I walked through the chaos with a message.
I was the lyric poet of grenades caught in the throat.
I visualized the outline of each catacomb.
I did not take sawdust to the hearts of the dictators.
I gathered the tears of all the mothers in a somber basin.
I served as a standard-bearer in the revolutions.
I loved a virgin girl.

I forced a cry of protest out of the sties.
I loved my friends with their feet firmly planted.
I was the child with no sieve.
I believed in a complete equality.
I was not a song but a cry of pain.
I had the scouring of bombs and bayonets for a mother tongue.
I closed myself in a bell jar to open my sad heart.
I was the metamorphosis of God.

I rummaged through the debris to rediscover purity.
I descended to the center of the earth to get the sunflower that
[was growing on its axis.
I discovered that the grains at the bottom of the sea are countless
[but very few know the way of the pearl.
I tried to go beyond and beneath the human context, but it was
[a mistake.
I looked for a wrecked airplane to build the house.
I invented a toy from the springs of a rusted tank.
I made a flower of barbed wire to carry into solitude.

Translated by **Richard Zenith**

## Das Circunstâncias do Poema

Não seja o poema
um pendão dobrado
na gaveta
da palavra dobrada

Não seja o poema
o joelho dobrado
nas circunstâncias
Ou exercício de si mesmo
em torre semântica
nem a palavra quebrada
antes do infinito

Não seja o poema
apenas a viagem
ao redor
do próprio corpo do poema
Nem o papel dobrado
no silêncio do bolso

Mas o exercício
corpo a corpo do poeta
entre uma dúvida e outra dúvida
mas dentro do horizonte
da certeza duvidada

Não seja igualmente
a inútil tragédia
escrita (desfraldada)
no inútil livro
do banco da escola
na boca do mundo

## On a Poem's Circumstances

Don't let the poem be
a pennant folded up
in the drawer
of the folded word

Don't let the poem be
the knee bent
to circumstances
Nor an exercise of itself
in a semantic tower
Nor the word broken
before the infinite

Don't let the poem be
a mere journey
around
the poem's own body
Nor paper folded up
in the silent pocket

But an exercise
—the poet's hand-to-hand combat—
between one and another doubt
(though always within the horizon
of doubted certainty)

Nor let it be
the useless tragedy
written (unfurled)
in the useless book
of the school desk
in the world's mouth

Não seja o poema
o perdão da humanidade
nem a aconchego da morte
Seja o poema
nos bancos da praça
e a vida
passada a sujo

Seja o poema a palavra subterrânea
Florida debaixo de terra própria,
jamais apropriada
A terra que a vida amansou
sem domar a vida

Seja o poema
a deflagração do homem
Seja o poema
o dobro da palavra poema
e mais que o dobro
para os que a consomem

A palavra emaranhada
na Teia de Tróia
A palavra passada a ferro
e dobrada de vinco diário
e arrancada do amário do medo
e da servidão

Seja o poema
o homem devorado pela luz
E seja a sebe sutil do tempo
onde encontrareis insetos e dúvidas
E mistério nenhum mais transparente
que a vida passada a limpo

Don't let the poem be
the forgiving of humanity
nor death's cozy comfort
Let the poem be
on the park bench
and life
soiled and dirty

Let the poem be the underground word
Flourishing beneath the earth itself,
never appropriated
The earth which life tilled
without quashing life

Let the poem be
man's flaming outburst
Let the poem be
more than the word poem
and more than that
for those who consume it

The word entangled
in the Web of the Net
The word ironed
and neatly folded every day
and pulled out of the cupboard of fear
and servitude

Let the poem be
man devoured by light
And let it be the hidden hedge of time
where you'll find insects and doubts
And no mystery more transparent
than life tidied and clean

Translated by **Richard Zenith**

## O Portão da Casa

Abri o portão.
        O coração rangeu.
                Rangeu
dentro de mim
e eu sorri
como um lavrador sorri
com seu rosto de terra
e a boca rasgada de riso
diante da terra lavrada.

Abri o portão partido. Partiu-me
em dois horizontes.
Em dois gomos de fruto fugaz.
Igual e desigual.

Abri o portão de minha casa.
E a ferrugem (ou seria orvalho?)
desatou o nó da palavra
pendurada por um fio
no fundo da garganta.

Abri o portão da casa de minha infância.
Mapa dobrado dentro de mim
desdobrado,
mapa mudo
onde afundei
em areia movediça
palavra por palavra.

Abri o portão da casa.
A boca do jardim, a travessia
do mundo.
O tempo fendeu
dentro e fora de onde vim
e espatifou as asas de papel
que vesti em mim.

## The House Gate

I opened the gate.
A heart creaked.
Creaked
inside me
and I smiled
as a tiller smiles
with his earthen face
and mouth wide open laughing
before the tilled land.

I opened the broken gate. It broke me
into two horizons.
Into two sections of a fleeting fruit.
Equal and unequal.

I opened the gate to my house.
And the rust (or was it dew?)
undid the knotted word
hanging by a thread
deep in my throat.

I opened the gate to my childhood house.
A folded map inside me
unfolded,
speechless map
where I sank
in quicksand
word by word.

I opened the house gate.
The garden entrance, the passage
to the world.
Time split
in and outside of where I came
and smashed the paper wings
I was wearing.

Manchei roupa, amor e ávidos tatos
em polpa de fruto proibido.
Poiu-se a pele nova na vivência,
no corpo dividido.
Entre sonhos, frêmitos, tristuras
e o real vivido.

Pois ainda que sonhe o tempo todo
ter o tempo de encontrar a verdade
em minhas mãos,
nada sei de mim
além de fotografias estampadas no jornal.
E pouca coisa mais saberei
ainda que acredite o contrário a cada instante
e que meu campo de batalha comigo mesmo
dure a vida inteira deste sonho
como dura o sonho a vida inteira
e, muitas vezes, se projete
além do horizonte aberto
do partão,
pouco mais ou nada mais
saberei.

A caixa vazia
de um velho relógio colonial
desliza sobre as águas do rio Itajaí-Açu
entre a lua cheia partida
e a nuvem veloz.

E todas estas palavras
e outras tantas nem escritas nem ditas
(esfacelada luz de uma estrela sem face nem foice)
fazem parte de minha biografia transparente.
Nada menos
nada mais.

I stained clothing, love and craving touch
with the juice of forbidden fruit.
The tender skin wore away from living in the world,
in my split body.
Among dreams, shivers, griefs
and life lived out.

For though I dream all the time
of having time to find truth
in my hands,
I know nothing of myself
beyond photos printed in the newspaper.
And I'll know little more
though every moment I believe the contrary,
and though the battle waged inside myself
will last the lifetime of this dream
even as the dream lasts a lifetime
and often extends
beyond the open horizon
of the gate,
little or nothing more
will I know.

The empty box
of an old colonial clock
glides over the waters of the natal river
between a broken full moon
and a swift cloud.

And all these words
and many others not written not spoken
(shattered light of a faceless scytheless star)
are part of my transparent biography.
Nothing less
nothing more.

Translated by **Richard Zenith**

## Da Esperança

O poema
(esta flor de luta perfeitíssima lótus)
cresce
onde em geral nada mais cresce.
Não carece de dinheiro
nem de honrarias.
Não aguarda promoções em cargo público
nem placa decerrada sob aplausos.

O poema cresce
no fundo da casa
para onde abre a janela basculante do banheiro.
Onde a cerca de estacas cai aos pedaços
apodrecida de esquecimento e pobreza.
Cresce no lugar mais distante
da admiração geral,
longe de movimentos literários
e de inventos passageiros.

Cresce o poema
sem adubos nem manifestos.
Integral em sua festa.
Sem técnicas aperfeiçoadas em redação de intrigas
ou resultado de anúncios cibernéticos.
Siquer tem parentesco
com diplomas emoldurados
de universidades brasileiras,
estrangeiras, interplanetárias, regionais.

Por ser destino crescer
cresce das cinzas do dia
e do lixo da humanidade.
É saliva ruminada de estábulos
e salas de visita.
É cuspe sorrateiro
na cabeça de códigos da ostentação.

## On Hope

The poem
(that flower of struggle most perfect lotus)
grows
where in general nothing else will.
It needs neither money
nor honors.
It awaits neither promotion in official standing
nor a plaque unveiled to thunderous applause.

The poem grows
at the back of the house
where the louvered bathroom window opens.
Where the picket fence is falling to pieces,
rotting from neglect and poverty.
It grows in a place far removed
from general admiration,
far from literary movements
and passing fashions.

The poem grows
without fertilizers or manifestoes.
Complete in its own celebration.
Without the perfected techniques of plot construction
or the latest cibernetic findings.
Nor has it the least kinship
with framed diplomas
from Brazilian universities
or from foreign, interplanetary, or regional ones.

Since its destiny is to grow
it grows from the daily ashes
and from the filth of humanity.
It is the cud chewed in stables
and living rooms.
It spits furtively
on the head of pompous behavior.

O poema se levanta
da riqueza recusada
por falta de habilidade e disfarce
no trato com as almas alheias.
E verde é seu tempo
onde para sempre
será vão guardar-se.

Cresce o poema de alguns milagres:
de refeição em refeição.
De reconciliação em reconciliação.
De amor perdido em amor achado.
De Deus fechar as portas todas
e deixar uma frestra
para a esperança do homem.
E das palavras, todas estas palavras
e suas metamorfoses
que atravessam o fundo da casa e o mundo
e as circunstâncias todas
que me atravessam.

The poem rises above
the wealth denied it
for lack of cunning and deception
in dealing with alien souls.
And green is its season
where it will forever
be futile to protect itself.

The poem grows from certain miracles:
from meal to meal.
From reconciliation to reconciliation.
From love lost to love found.
From God closing all doors
but leaving a crack
open for man's hope.
And from words, all these words
and their metamorphoses
that cross at the back of the house and of the world
and all the circumstances
by which I am crossed.

Translated by **William Jay Smith**

## Minifúndio

Sem limites intransponíveis.
Nem infinitos
ne minifúndio.
A terra persiste
e o homem permanece
matéria de tudo.

Não há velocidade de luz escrita
nem ensinada
no minifúndio.
Os olhos do lavrador
iluminam a terra
e guardam o dia sob pálpebras e rugas
quando dorme.
E caminha torto no sonho
como torto caminha na vida.

Pesares, tristuras.
Fértil celebração das circunstâncias.
Não há enigmas
nem ambigüidades feitas de ausência
no minifúndio.
Tudo é redondo:
curiosidade, espanto, laços de família,
esplendores de pouca futilidade.

Não se vai a lugar nenhum
sem carregar a moita de mistério.
O minifúndio se faz
na terra da palavra.

Enterrem-me na palavra.

## Small Farm

No limits are impassable.
Nor infinite
on the small farm.
The land persists
and man remains
the substance of all things.

The speed of light is neither written
nor taught
on the small farm.
The farmer's eyes
light up the land
and guard the day under wrinkled eyelids
while he sleeps.
He walks crooked in his dreams
as a crooked man walks in life.

Griefs, sorrows.
Fertile celebration of circumstances.
No enigmas
nor ambiguities wrought from absence
on the small farm.
All is round:
curiosity, fright, family ties,
splendors with little futility.

No one goes anywhere
without carrying with him the hush of mystery.
The small farm is born
in the land of the word.

Bury me in the word.

Translated by **Richard Zenith**

## Desterro

Aqui estou eu
em pleno século XX
desterrado por Platão.
Dentro do círculo da vida
não mais aberto
que um não.

Que faço neste tempo
entre terra a céu de ironia?
Em coração caracol
e tempo de uvas verdes?

Faço um poema.
Me desfaço.
Me desfaço como um laço
de uma caixa de presentes vazia.

E enquanto me desfaço no poema
afino o sentimento do mundo:
desterro se faz de nenhum lugar.
E só se faz de saudade.

## Exile

Here I am
in the mid-20th century
exiled by Plato.
Inside life's circle
no more open
than a no.

What shall I do in this season
between earth and ironic heaven?
In a spiraling heart
and a season of green grapes?

I put together a poem.
I take myself apart.
I undo myself like a string
from a box emptied of presents.

And while I come apart in the poem
I tune in to world feeling:
exile comes from nowhere.
It comes only from homesickness.

Translated by **Richard Zenith**

## Deste Âmago Provo o Amargo Gosto

Deste âmago provo o amargo gosto.
Antigo fruto exposto.
De saudade.

Deste amargo provo
o gosto amargo de ser aos poucos
não mais que discernimento,
lúcido epitáfio, esquecimento.

Quem sabe este amargo seja sangue.
Quem sabe este gosto vem da água.
Quem sabe de vinagre, quem sabe de mágua.
Quem sabe este amargo seja terra.
Quem sabe a tudo sabe
por tudo ser de amargura.

Não importa.
Eu provo este amargo gosto
como um rosto
que se olha por fascinação
mas também por desgosto.

Eu provo o amargo gosto deste rosto.
E amo o que provo
pelo amargo gosto.

## Of This Core I Sample the Bitter Taste

Of this core I sample the bitter taste.
The taste of old fruit exposed.
                    To yearning.

Of this bitterness I sample
the bitter taste of slowly becoming
no more than a discernment,
a lucid epitaph, a part of oblivion.

Who knows if this bitterness is blood.
Who knows if this taste comes from water.
Or from vinegar or from grief.
Or if this bitterness is the earth.
Who knows knows everything
for everything tastes of bitterness.

No matter.
I sample this bitterness
like a face
that gazes at itself with fascination
and also with disgust.

I sample the bitter taste of this face.
And I love what I sample
                    for its bitter taste.

Translated by **William Jay Smith**

## Do Tempo

Serei breve.
Mas não tão breve
que a eternidade
escape do coração.

Porque sobre a terra
cresce um sonho
de grão em grão
até a plenitude.
É meu sonho, de terra justa
e perfeita
e dividida.

Cresce
enquanto espero e cresço
E me acresço
de vão em vão
até o tempo inteiro, o tempo interior,
em terra de romã e sonho justo
e perfeito
e dividido.

Serei breve.
Mas não tão breve
que a eternidade
escape do coração.

## On Time

I'll be brief.
But not so brief
that eternity
escape the heart.

Because over the land
a dream
bit by bit
grows to its full.
It's my dream: of a just land
perfect
and shared by all.

It grows
while I wait and grow.
and I grow
little by little
to an entire time, an interior time
in the land of the pomegranate and the just dream
perfect
and shared by all.

I'll be brief.
But not so brief
that eternity
escape the heart.

Translated by **William Jay Smith**

## O Poema do Telhado de Vidro

Estende a mão
contra o vidro
da sala onde sonhas.
Joga também o coração
se for teu
e não for um cálice
de veneno diário.

Estende a mão
em direção do próximo
como se fosse
a coluna matinal de um diário
que se lê, diariamente,
para lembrar
o estar aqui o ser
e, mais do que nunca,
a duras penas,
e ainda assim suave
como as linhas de uma colina verde
aqui estar.

Quebra o vidro do telhado
da tua casa
(ou será tua causa?).
O vidro do telhado de vidro.
O vidro do telhado do vizinho
e do vizinho mais próximo
e, também, mais distante, provavelmente.
O telhado de vidro das casas da tua rua
do bairro de vidro onde moras, da tua cidade,
o mundo inteiro e seus telhados de vidro

e deixa a sala do sonho
para catar um tempo
fora dos vidros.

## The Glass-Roof Poem

Reach out your hand
against the glass
of the room you dream in.
Toss the heart in too
if it's yours
and not a chalice
of daily poison.

Reach out your hand
toward your fellow man
as if he were
the morning newspaper column
which is read daily
to remember
that life is here now
and, as never before,
at great pains,
and yet it's gentle
as the lines of a green hill
to be here now.

Break the glass in the roof
of your house
(or is it your cause?).
The glass of the glass roof.
The glass of your neighbor's roof
and of your closest neighbor
and probably also the most distant.
The glass roof of the houses on your street,
in the glass neighborhood where you live, in your city,
the whole world and its glass roofs

and leave the room you dream in
to search for a time
outside the glass.

O sonho fora da sala
é senha deste tempo.
Carrego na mala
de meu passatempo.

E cada vez mais amplo
se faz o pensamento
de estar e ser
(estarrecer)
ao mesmo tempo
dentro e fora
da sala do tempo.

Deixa entrar na sala
o tempo da sala de fora.
Pouse na testa franzida
e sobre teu sonho franzino
de quebrar a idéia geral do mundo
e, a duras penas, conhecer
as linhas da vida
que a mão encerra.
As mesmas linhas fundas
que vincam a terra.

Saber de terra
o cheiro da chuva
e como é bom sujar os pés.
E que a vida
é vidro quebrado
que o corpo recolherá
como uma dádiva
entre as trevas.

Ah! Coração, vão de passagem!
Quebrado
dentro e fora de si.
            Fora e dentro
da sala.
            Fora e dentro
da vida.

The dream outside the room
is the password of the times.
I carry it in my bag
of pastimes.

And the thought
of being and being here
(being here in fear)—
is always getting larger
at the same time
inside and outside
the room of time.

Let into the room
the time from the outside room.
Let it rest on your frowning brow
and over your delicate dream
of breaking the general idea of the world
and, at great pains, knowing
the lines of life
that your hand holds.
The same deep lines
which furrow the earth.

To know earth
the smell of rain
and how good it is to dirty your feet.
To know that life
is broken glass
which the body will gather
like manna
in the darkness.

Ah! Heart, gateway!
Broken
inside and outside itself.
                Outside and inside
the room.
                Outside and inside
life.

Navegar é destino
entre os telhados de vidro
como um gato aceso, lânguido,
sozinho.
Revelar as linhas d'água fogo d'horizonte
que só a luz revela,
sonho multiplicado, multificado,
multiferido,

mil pétalas de dor espalhadas
espelhadas na lua
sobre os telhados de vidro,
o corpo felino,
            perplexo, transitório,
o pulsar do tempo
mais curto que a mais curta distância,
sob a sombra de uma árvore de papel,
de mentira,
ao cair da tarde,
ao cair da manhã,
enfeixado no meu tempo na sala
fora da sala,

flexível,
flechável,
quebrado vidro
no meio de um filme projetado
no perpétuo cinema chamado viver,

escura sala de nenhuma diferença
nem de igualdade nenhuma,
infinitamente através dos vidros
desfocado,
desfolhado em versos inúteis
em vulgar solilóquia estrela do mar.

To sail is destiny
among the glass roofs
like a cat on fire, languid,
alone.
To reveal the water's lines horizon's fire
which only light reveals,
dream multiplied, mummified,
mutilated,

a thousand petals of pain scattered
shimmering in the moon
over the glass roofs,
the feline body,
                    uncertain, transitory,
the pulsing beat of time
shorter than the shortest distance,
under the shade of a paper tree,
all lies,
as it falls in the evening,
as it falls in the morning,
tied up in my time in the room
outside the room,

flexible,
vulnerable,
broken glass
in the midst of a film being shown
in the perpetual cinema called living,

a dark room with no difference
nor similarity,
infinitely through the glasses
unfocused,
disfoliated in useless verses
in a trivial soliloquy star of the sea.

Aqui estou no meu lugar comum, no meu lugar.
Carne, osso,
e, sobretudo, devaneio.
A roupa de fora
igual à roupa de dentro.
A sala de dentro do mundo
igual à sala do mundo de fora.
O tempo semelhante
à própria dissemelhança.

E o sonho? Ah! O sonho!
Um gato sobre os telhados de vidro,
aceso, lânguido,
sozinho,
trincado, truncado,
circunscrito,
espatifado,

no mundo inteiro
um sonho
sobre os telhados de vidro.

Here I am in my common place, in my place.
Flesh, bone,
and, above all, daydream.
Outer clothing
just like inner clothing.
The room inside the world
just like the room of the outside world.
Time similar
to dissimilarity itself.

And the dream? Ah, the dream!
A cat atop the glass roofs,
burning, languid,
alone,
scratched, mutilated,
delimitated,
shattered,

in the whole world
one dream
atop the glass roofs.

Translated by **Richard Zenith**

# BIBLIOGRAPHY


JORGE MAUTNER

*Deus da Chuva e da Morte* (1962); *Kaos* (1963); *Narciso em Tarde Cinza* (1965); *Jorge, o Vigarista* (1965); *Fragmentos de Sabonete* (1976); *Panfletos da Nova Era* (1980); *Poesias de Amor e de Morte* (1982).

FERREIRA GULLAR

Poetry: *A Luta Corporal* (1954); *Poemas* (1958); *Dentro da Noite Veloz* (1975); *Poema Sujo* (1977); *Na Vertigem do Dia* (1980); *Toda Poesia* (1980). Plays: *Se Correr o Bicho Pega, Se Ficar o Bicho Come* (1966); *A Saída, Onde Está a Saída?* (1967); *Dr. Getúlio, Sua Vida e Sua Glória* (1968); *Um Rubi no Umbigo* (1978). Essays: *Teoria do Não Objeto* (1959); *Cultura Posta em Questão* (1965); *Vanguarda e Subdesenvolvimento* (1969).

HAROLDO DE CAMPOS

Poetry: *Auto do Possesso* (1950); *Antologia de Poemas* in *Noigandres* 5 (1962); *Servidão de Passagem* (1962); *Xadrez de Estrelas* (1976); *Signatia: Quasi Coelum* (1979). Essays: *Revisão de Sousândrade* (with Augusto de Campos) (1964); *Teoria da Poesia Concreta* (with Augusto de Campos and Décio Pignatari (1965); *Sousândrade-Poesia* (with Augusto de Campos) (1966); *A Arte no Horizonte do Provável* (1969); *Morfologia do Macunaíma* (1973); *Metalinguagem* (1976); *A Operação do Texto* (1976); *Ruptura dos Gêneros na LIteratura Latino-Americana* (1977). Translations of Dante, Pound, Joyce, Mallarmé, Mayakovsky, and Khlebnikov.

MÁRIO FAUSTINO

Poetry: *Poesia de Mário Faustino,* with an introduction by Benedito Nunes (1966). Essays: *Mário Faustino—Cinco Ensaios Sobre Poesia,* with an introduction by Assis Brasil (1964); *Mário Faustino—Poesia-Experiência,* with an introduction by Benedito Nunes (1976).

# BIBLIOGRAPHY


## AUGUSTO DE CAMPOS

Poetry: *O Rei Menos O Reino* (1951); *Ad Augustum per Angusta* and *O Sol por Natural* in *Noigandres* 1 (1952); *Poetamenos* in *Noigandres* 2 (1955); *Ovonovelo* in *Noigandres* 3 (1956); concrete poems in *Noigandres* 4 (1958); selected poems in *Noigandres* 5 (1962); concrete poems in *Invenção* 2 to 5 (1962–1967); *Luxo* (1967); *Poema-Objeto* in *Objetos* de Julio Plaza (1969); *Equivocábulos* (1970); *Linguaviagem* (1970); *Colidouescapo* (1971); *Viva Vaia* (1972); *Profilograma 2 ((hom' cage to webern,* a postcard poem) (1972); *Poetamenos* (second edition) (1973); *Poemóbiles* (Object poems) (with Julio Plaza) (1974); *Caixa Preta* (an intersemiotic collection of poems, objects, and object-poems, with Julio Plaza) (1975); *Segredos d'Alma—Augusto de Campos —Versos 1926* (a ready-made book-poem) (1978); *Poesia 1949–1979 (Viva Vaia)* (1979). Essays: *Revisão de Sousândrade* (with Haroldo de Campos) (1964); *Teoria de Poesia concreta* (with Haroldo de Campos and Décio Pignatari (1965); *Sousândrade—Poesia* (with Haroldo de Campos) (1966). Translations of Cavalcanti, Dante, John Donne, e. e. cummings, Ezra Pound, James Joyce, Mallarmé, and others.

## DÉCIO PIGNATARI

Poetry: *Poesia Pois é Poesia* (collected poems) (1977). Essays: *Informação, Linguagem, Comunicação* (1968); *Contra-comunicação* (1971); *Semiótica e Literatura* (1974); *Comunicação Poética* (1977); *Semiótica da Arte e da Arquitetura* (1980).

## LINDOLF BELL

*Os Postomos e as Profecias* (1962); *Os Ciclos* (1964); *Convocação* (1965); *Antologia Poética de Lindolf Bell* (1965); *Curta Primavera* (poetical narrative) (1966); *A Tarefa* (1967); *As Annamárias* (1971); *Catequese Poética* (anthology) (1968); *As Vivências Elementares* (1981).

# NOTES ON EDITORS AND TRANSLATORS

**EMANUEL BRASIL**, born in 1940 in Rio de Janeiro, is a Brazilian novelist, critic, and teacher of modern dance. He is the author of *Ghost Stone (Pedra Fantasma),* a novel, published in 1977. In 1972 with Elizabeth Bishop he compiled *An Anthology of Twentieth Century Brazilian Poetry* (Wesleyan University Press), and in 1978 was guest editor of the Brazilian number of *The Literary Review* (Fairleigh Dickinson University). He studied law and psychology, and since 1965 has lived in New York, where he has been a translator for the United Nations and editor at Vanguard Press. In 1969 he received a grant from the Ingram Merrill Foundation. His new novel *History of Brazil (Historia do Brasil 1954–1964)* is scheduled for publication in 1983.

**JEAN R. LONGLAND**, Curator of the Library of the Hispanic Society of America, has had a distinguished career as a translator of Spanish, Portuguese, and Brazilian poetry. She has received translation prizes in 1970 and 1974 from *Poet Lore;* the Portugal Prize in 1973 of the International Poetry Association and the Portuguese government; and in 1974 the Membership Medal of the Hispanic Society of America. She edited and translated *Selections from Contemporary Portuguese Poetry* (1966). Since 1977 as Vice President of the American Portuguese Society, she has been a panelist and guest lecturer at various translation conferences. She is currently translating the work of Fernando Pessoa and Egito Gonçalves, and is collaborating with Luciana Stegagno Picchio on a Portuguese-English anthology of medieval Galician-Portuguese poetry.

**ROMNEY MEYRAN**, poet and translator, was born in 1950 in Los Angeles. He is the author of the chapbook *Sahaja, Poetry of Love* and of *Rain Down America,* as yet unpublished.

**EDWIN MORGAN** was born in 1920 in Glasgow, where he is Senior Lecturer in English at Glasgow University. He is the author of *The Cape of Good Hope* (1955), *The Second Life* (1967), and of several volumes of concrete poetry. His verse translation of *Beowulf* appeared in 1967. His work is represented in the *Oxford Book of Scottish Verse* (1966), *Modern Scottish Poetry* (1966), and other anthologies. His translation of "Transient Servitude" of Haroldo de Campos is from his book *Rites of Passage* (1976).

## NOTES ON EDITORS AND TRANSLATORS

WILLIAM JAY SMITH, poet, critic, and translator, is the author of eight books of poetry, two of which were final contenders for the National Book Award. In 1980 he published three books: *The Traveler's Tree: New and Selected Poems*, *Army Brat: A Memoir*, and *Laughing Time: Nonsense Poems* (a selection of his children's poems). Mr. Smith has translated poetry from French, Italian, Spanish, Portuguese, Russian, Swedish, and Hungarian. A former Consultant in Poetry to the Library of Congress (1968–1970), he has received many honors, including in 1972 the Loines Award from the American Academy and Institute of Arts and Letters, which elected him a member in 1975, the Gold Medal of Labor from the Hungarian government in 1978, and the Golden Rose from the New England Poetry Club in 1979. He spent the first six months of 1980 as a Fulbright Lecturer in Moscow and Belgrade.

RICHARD ZENITH, born in 1956 in Washington, D.C., studied at the University of Virginia and Columbia University. A poet and translator, he is currently living in Brazil, where he is teaching English and completing his first novel.

## NOTES ABOUT THE BOOK

The text and display type are Helvetica. Composition and typesetting were done by Carolinatype of Durham, N.C. The book was printed on 60 lb Springhill Offset paper and bound in Holliston Roxite by Kingsport Press, Kingsport, Tennessee.
Design and production were by Joyce Kachergis Book Design & Production, Bynum, North Carolina.